'Stella Gibney's memoir, *It Will* who has suffered more trauma and upheaval in her life than most . . . Through her lifelong habit of journaling, Stella Gibney has been able to come through the toughest of times and arrive at new beginnings with a positivity that I admired to the end . . . *It Will Get Better* is a raw and honest account of a working class girl growing up in the 1960s and 70s in New Zealand . . . if you enjoy a memoir then I suggest you give this a go, it starts off with a bang, grabs you and then shows you how life can get better.'   *That Book You Like*

'. . . the stories of Stella's life aren't pleasant or even easy but she writes them with total grace and humanity. It is her simple and honest delivery that makes it so readable, and ultimately far less harrowing than it must have been to live through.'   *Create Hope Inspire*

'This is a simple account of a life spent overcoming problems, yet it's a life lived well and always with optimism.'   *Good Reading*

'. . . unlike her brothers and sisters, Stella suffered a number of abusive incidents during her formative years. But Stella was determined not to let years of horrific abusive situations and domestic violence determine her life. She found solace in writing her thoughts down in a series of journals. Through writing she began to understand her feelings and how to gain control of her life . . . This is her inspiring story of reclaiming her life and creating a happy home for herself and her two boys.'

Mildura Midweek

'*It Will Get Better* is the inspirational true story of one woman's courage to overcome abuse and heartache to create a better life.'   *Femail*

STELLA GIBNEY

It Will Get Better

ALLEN&UNWIN

SYDNEY · MELBOURNE · AUCKLAND · LONDON

This book is dedicated to my wonderful sons,
Josh, Jem and Corey.

Names have been changed to protect privacy.

This edition published in 2015

Copyright © Stella Gibney 2014

Allen & Unwin
Sydney, Melbourne, Auckland, London

83 Alexander Street
Crows Nest NSW 2065
Australia
Phone: (61 2) 8425 0100
Fax: (61 2) 9906 2218
Email: info@allenandunwin.com
Web: www.allenandunwin.com

Cataloguing-in-Publication details are available
from the National Library of Australia
trove.nla.gov.au

ISBN 978 1 92526 622 1

Set in Granjon by Bookhouse, Sydney
Text design by Alissa Dinallo
Printed and bound in Australia by Griffin Press

10 9 8 7 6 5 4 3 2 1

Foreword

It was a warm sunny Saturday morning as I sat alongside my sister Stella outside our rented house overlooking the sea near Sydney's Whale Beach. Palm Beach, just up the road, was the place that Stella had called home for over fifteen years and we talked about how much she loved living near the ocean. I had only been a Sydney convert for a few years, having moved from Tasmania with my husband Richard and son Zac. We relocated to Sydney when I was offered the role of Julie Rafter in *Packed to the Rafters* and had been staying in the Eastern Suburbs when Stella suggested we look for a place on Sydney's Northern Beaches. We immediately saw why Stella loved the lifestyle and I understood why this was where Stella had decided to finally put down roots after a life spent moving from place to place. It also meant that we as sisters could spend more time together—something that had been missing for many years as we lived in different states and had very different lives. The great thing about our family is that no matter how long we spend apart we always come together as if the years have fallen away, picking up where we left off. It is this ability to live in the present that I think has made our journeys and our struggles a little easier to overcome. However, I have always been amazed at Stella's particular ability to see the positive in any situation, given that she endured a very difficult start to life.

We were discussing this that morning when I noticed that Stella seemed preoccupied. I asked her what was wrong and she said that she just felt a little sad. Both her boys were now grown and had moved into their own homes. She was in a job that although she enjoyed, she felt that there was something missing in her life. I remembered that she used to write in a journal whenever she felt sad and I asked her if she still did so. That in turn sparked a conversation that would lead to this book.

Stella wanted to leave a legacy of her life. I asked her where were all the journals she had kept over the years and she remarked that she still had them all.

'Why don't you write a book then?' People have often asked me to write my autobiography, but for me the timing hasn't been right. However, I knew that my sister had a story to be told and I wanted to encourage her to do so. I picked up the phone, called my agent and asked if she could put us in touch with a publisher. In turn the publisher asked for a few pages of Stella's writing. Stella wasn't even sure if she could do it. Writing a journal is one thing, but a book? Could her years of journalling be condensed and crafted into a story sharing the feelings in her heart, a story that would make people want to turn the pages? The only way to find out was to simply sit down and write. And she did. Page after page of my sister's story poured out of her. Our colourful and often dysfunctional childhood, the pain of being taken as a child, the sexual abuse, finding love and losing love, raising two boys single-handedly, starting her own business only to see that taken away, and having her faith tested so that one day she found herself staring at the very ocean she loved and wondering if that's where it all should end.

I know my sister Stella is worried that she may not be a writer and that people may not even read this book. She is concerned that her recollections may differ from those of the people she writes about. But, most importantly, she is worried that she may hurt people with her words. That's my sister in a nutshell. She will always put other people first. For me, this book is my sister's legacy. It is an opportunity to tell her story in her own words. Of course there will be times when her recollections differ from the way other people remember things. Our memories do that to us. She has admitted that there are places where she has had to fill in the gaps. None of us can say we remember everything that happened in our lives with absolute clarity, and in some ways I think that is a gift.

And so here is my sister's story. I know that her one wish is to help even one person cope a little better by sharing her life's experiences with them. If she can achieve that then her dream will have come true.

Stella's theory is if you have a notepad and a pen then you have a friend. By getting it out of your head and onto a page it is as if an invisible force is listening. Some people call this God. Others call it the witness: the still, quiet voice inside that is always there, understanding, and reminding you that you are never alone. I know I believe that. I also believe that we are all connected in some way and, by sharing our stories of love and loss, pain and joy, we can help each other through life's wonderful journey.

My sister Stella is a magnificent human being whom I love dearly. I know that this book is the beginning of yet another wonderful season in her life.

Rebecca Gibney

Preface

I have experienced many painful events throughout my life, from abduction and childhood sexual abuse to teenage pregnancy, two failed marriages and bankruptcy. During it all I have found healing and forgiveness through my faith in God and through expressing myself via my notepad and pen, which became my closest companions.

I began journalling when I was in my early twenties. It was my secret, a place I went to share my innermost thoughts and feelings that no one knew of. From the joys of childbirth and raising children to hidden pain buried deep inside the child in me.

When I picked up my pen and began to write I wasn't alone. There was always someone there to listen, someone to understand. I knew if I could get it down on paper it would help me heal. Many of my journals are tear-stained and full of painful memories. Countless times I had to seek counselling to heal the damaged child inside, but it was worth it.

Over the years I have filled fifteen journals covering every season in my life, from the good times to the bad. Through them all I have learned the most valuable lesson of all: who I am. After years of trying to be the person I thought everyone else needed me to be, I am finally free to be myself, and that feels good.

As a single mum, for a number of years I found it difficult to get my sons to express their feelings when I knew they were sad or upset. I remember asking them when they were very young if they couldn't tell me their troubles maybe they could write them down or draw them in a picture. I knew from my own experience how much it helped me and I hoped it would help them too. It was often painful uncovering emotions of hurt and rejection through a simple drawing or described in a letter, but it was healing for them. It helped us all to understand what was really going on inside their hearts and minds. Today we have a closeness that I believe began many years ago through sharing our pain and struggles together. I am so very proud of them for that.

My mantra has always been it's just a season, it will get better. I hope you enjoy sharing my journey.

Letter from Jem

Reading through the pages that follow has been, for my part, both a prideful and a painful experience. Painful because it has entailed reading of the hardships my mother has unfortunately had to endure (many of which I was unaware of); prideful because I read these pages with the knowledge that the woman who recounts them has not let an often tumultuous life get the better of her.

To live through everything my mum has, and manage to remain a joyous and loving person, is no small feat. And to be willing to share it all so candidly with anyone that reads this takes an openness to which I personally aspire. Such openness in the writing that follows is representative of what I take to be one of the book's main pieces of advice: that writing is a powerful form of release when you have nowhere else to turn.

As socially embedded, necessarily dependent creatures, at some point everyone feels the need to express their emotions to those around them. As a shy and introverted child, I possibly felt this compulsion less than others, and certainly less than others in my family. Writing my thoughts and feelings down (as my mum encouraged me to do) was, I remember, a far more comfortable way of sharing what I was too shy or embarrassed to express verbally. What's more, in forcing fragmented thoughts and emotions into the structured form of written sentences, I found myself trying to make sense of why I felt a certain way. The articulation of my feelings was, even before (or without) sharing them, an illuminating and therapeutic experience.

I have no kids as yet, so, despite having a great role model, I will not pretend to know how to raise them. However, I will say that writing has been a form of therapy that I would recommend to any parent with a child hesitant as I was to express their emotions in person. Likewise for anyone going through, as my mother would have it, one of those seasons in which everything just goes from bad to worse.

Of course, writing (or drawing) won't fix everything, nor will it even fix some things for everyone. But for my part, I have little doubt that early encouragements to express my emotions in written form were both cathartic for myself as well as enlightening for my struggling single mum.

As a final note I'd like to say a personal thankyou to my mum. Josh and myself are who we are today because you instilled in us the persistent belief that circumstances, like seasons, will change. Yet through everything detailed here, you've managed to remain the same honest, loving and reliable mother. For that I'm grateful beyond words.

Your son and, more importantly, your friend,
Jem

Letter from Josh
My mum has taught me many things throughout my life. She has taught me the importance of truly listening to people,

to treat others the way I would want them to treat me, as well as other morals that I still live by.

Mum also showed me how to express my feelings. From a young age I learnt how to understand and manage my emotions and why it is so vital to do so. Sometimes she would encourage me to write it all down; if I couldn't write it she would suggest I draw a picture. It wasn't easy; in fact it was usually very hard and nearly always made me upset. However, by doing this I was able to recognise how I was feeling and what triggered my sadness or anger.

Understanding myself in this way has not only helped me grow as a person, it has helped enormously in my relationships with others, particularly with my fiancée. For this quality I am forever thankful.

Love,
Josh

Chapter One

It was another ordinary day in the small New Zealand town of Masterton. I had gone across the road to the milk bar to buy a loaf of bread. As I came out of the shop to cross the road, an old pale blue van pulled up in front of me. A man with greying hair leaned across the passenger seat and flung open the side door. 'Come here, little girl,' he said.

I came closer, used to doing what I was told.

'Would you like a chocolate ice cream?' the man asked.

I don't know why I climbed into the front seat of the pale blue van that day. Mum had always taught us never to speak to strangers. Perhaps it was the promise of ice cream, a rare treat for us in those days.

As the van pulled out onto the road, I sat quietly, trying to be a good girl. We drove to the other end of town and the man stopped outside a small corner shop. He didn't say a word to me, just got out of the van, walked into the store and returned with the biggest ice cream I had ever seen. It was double choc-dipped, my favourite. I took a bite, relieved that he'd done as he'd promised—he must be a nice man, who was going to take me home now.

But he began driving in the opposite direction from my house. It was growing dark and I started to feel scared. Where was he taking me? Why were we going the wrong way? I began to cry. 'I want to go home. Please take me home. I want my mummy.' He didn't say a word.

He drove several miles out of town until we came to a lonely stretch of road lined with pine trees. There were no other cars in sight. He pulled the van to a stop beneath the pines and turned off the ignition. What was he stopping for? What was he going to do to me?

'Get in the back,' he demanded. Those four words would haunt me for many years to come.

Shaking with fear, begging, 'Please don't hurt me', I scrambled over the front seat and onto a dirty old mattress that lined the back of the van. Stained curtains yellowing with age covered the small back windows.

I lay down and started crying again. 'I want my mummy, I want to go home, please take me home.' He opened the back door and climbed inside.

I cried throughout the ordeal. 'I want my mummy, I want my mummy.' Until finally it was over.

The man moved away from me and opened the back door, telling me to climb into the front. I was shaking and in shock.

He started up the van and drove back towards town. On the outskirts, near a small cluster of shops, he stopped and told me to get out. It was dark and the shops were closed up for the night. My legs were sore and I felt sick as I began the long walk back to the other end of town. I huddled as close as I could to the shop fronts, trying to be invisible, afraid he would come back for me. All I wanted was my mum, but I was scared she would be cross with me. I had been gone for a long time and everything that had happened had been my fault because I had got into that van. What was I going to tell her?

I trudged along slowly, quietly crying, when I noticed a group of people in the distance, and then someone came running towards me. It was my mum. I was so happy to see her. She picked me up in her arms and held me close. 'Where have you been? We've been so worried about you.' The whole family had been out looking for me, and the police too.

'I'm okay, nothing happened, Mum, truly. I just went for a drive with a man who bought me an ice cream. I'm so sorry.' I began to cry.

At home Mum sat me down and, asking my brother to look after me, said she would be back in a minute. I didn't worry about where she had gone, I was just so happy to be home. She returned after a moment, saying she wanted me to get into my pyjamas. She helped me take off my clothes and get ready for bed, then she left the room again, only to return and say we had to go for a drive. I learnt later that the police had asked Mum to examine my clothes, and in doing so she had found bloodstains on my underwear.

A police car was waiting outside. Suddenly I was scared again. I was a bad girl for getting in the van. The police probably thought it was my fault. I kept saying, 'I'm so sorry. Please don't be angry with me.' Mum's response was to hold me tight and reassure me.

At the police station I was taken to a room and asked to climb onto the bed, where a police doctor would examine me. Mum wasn't allowed in the room with me. I was bewildered and afraid; I didn't want anyone to touch me again. The doctor confirmed I had been sexually assaulted. In another room a policeman sat me down in front of coloured pens and paper and asked me to draw a picture of the man. He was old, with grey hair and very hairy arms; that was all I could remember. I was asked to draw a picture of the van, which I remembered vividly. It was pale blue, with no windows on the sides but two small windows at the back with those dirty yellowing curtains.

The following day Mum and I had to go for another drive, this time to show the police where the man had taken me. I knew exactly where it had been, because I would never forget the tall pine trees that loomed over the road when the van stopped. Fresh tyre tracks in the dirt confirmed the location.

Within a matter of days, the police had arrested the man responsible. A teenage boy had seen him trying to coerce his sister into the pale blue van the very same day I'd been abducted. Thinking quickly, the boy had recorded the registration number before racing to his sister's aid, then he'd called the police.

Before he was due to go to trial, the man admitted himself to a mental institution to avoid the hearing. When he was eventually brought to trial, Mum went to the court and heard his lawyer argue that the assault had not been premeditated and had been his first offence. He stood in the dock, his wife and two teenage daughters in the gallery. To my mum and dad's disgust, he was sentenced to a mere eighteen months in prison for the sexual assault of a six-year-old girl.

Chapter Two

I don't remember much of my life before that fateful day when I was six years old. Mum said I was a quiet little girl and very shy. Maybe being the second to youngest of six kids might have had something to do with it.

My dad was from a large Irish Catholic family, so it was no surprise that Mum had five little ones before she was twenty-four. Michael was born when Mum was just eighteen, then came Teresa, Patrick, Diana and me; four and a half years later, my younger sister Rebecca was born. We were quite poor when we were growing up. Dad was a drycleaner. It didn't pay much, and it was hard with so many little mouths to feed. I don't know how my mum coped in the early years. She had five children under the age of six at home, with no washing machine. She had to wash our nappies in the bath. We didn't go on family holidays, or have expensive birthday or Christmas presents, although Mum would always make sure there was something for us to open. We didn't have money for new clothes, so we wore hand-me-downs or shared our clothes.

Looking back, it didn't matter that we didn't have nice things; we had each other and we shared a closeness that a lot of other families don't have. Maybe that was because we shared a secret: the shame of having an abusive alcoholic father.

Dad had always been a drinker, but in the first year of married life, his drinking spiralled out of control and he became violent. The smallest thing—a messy cupboard, a meal without green vegetables—would set him off into an angry rage. His nickname for Mum was 'Stupid'. It's hardly surprising she struggled with low self-esteem for many years of her life.

One day, when he was three years old, Patrick witnessed something no child should ever have to see. It was late on a Saturday night. Mum had put Michael, Teresa, Patrick and Diana to bed. Dad had been drinking heavily all day, as he always did every weekend. First came the verbal abuse, then came the violence. Dad was on a rampage; he began chasing Mum around the house. Fearing for her life, she ran to the kitchen to call the police. As she grabbed the phone, Dad came running up behind her. My brother Patrick had been woken by Mum's screams for help. 'Mummy!' he cried out as he toddled into the kitchen to find Dad looming over Mum with a knife. Dad swung around and, seeing his little boy crying in the doorway, dropped the knife in shame.

Dad wasn't always drunk. He would drink during the week, but would save the binging for weekends. He always denied that he was an alcoholic because of this; he thought he could control his drinking. During the week he was relatively quiet, and a gentle man with a great sense of humour. On Sundays, before his drinking started in earnest, we would sit around the lunch table for 'quiz time'. I was never very good at answering the questions Dad pulled out of the paper, so I would keep quiet while Diana and Patrick competed against each other for the most correct answers. Dad called them the Bobsy Twins because they were so alike. After lunch was the Sunday matinee on TV. When most kids were outside playing, we were inside with the curtains drawn watching the midday movie. The best part of the afternoon was when the movie was over. We would go out onto the verandah where we were each given a large slice of cold watermelon and a sheet of newspaper to spit the pips onto. Sometimes Dad would watch us play cricket in the backyard. He'd been a very good fast bowler in his youth and had taught us the game. These are happy memories of my father, and I hold them close to my heart because they were so rare in my younger years.

As children we didn't discuss our situation among ourselves, however we never invited friends over. The abuse was a secret that we kept between us.

I don't have any memories of achieving anything significant as a child. I wasn't any good at sports and I wasn't very clever. Looking back, I think I felt like I had failed Mum and Dad. One incident in particular stands out for me. One of the few things we did as a family was to watch the little athletics in the local park. My sister Diana was a good runner and she competed in the hundred-metre sprint. I didn't like running and was happy to sit on the sideline cheering her on. The day before one particular athletics carnival Mum told me that Dad wanted me to run in the fifty-metre sprint the next day. I was terrified. 'I'm no good at running, Mum. Please don't make me,' I pleaded, but when Dad decided something, Mum never argued.

The next day arrived all too quickly. When my race was called, I dragged my feet to the start and lined up with the other seven year olds. My legs were shaking and my heart was racing. I was terrified. My fear was of failing and of disappointing my father. I felt as though I needed to go to the toilet. I squeezed my legs together, trying to hold on, but suddenly I felt the trickle of wee running down my legs. Just then I heard the call, 'Ready . . . . Steady . . . Go!' The other girls launched themselves from the start line. I set off after them, but I was trying to hold my legs together so no one would see I had wet myself. The race was over and I was barely halfway down the track. Embarrassed and ashamed, I shuffled over to the sideline. I felt like an utter failure. I had let Dad down. I was no good at anything at all.

•

By the time I was eight years old we had moved house four times. Mum and Dad couldn't afford to buy a place of their own, so we lived in rental properties, all of them old and rundown.

When we moved from Masterton to Hastings, we rented a big, rambling house that had been built in the early 1900s. It was on a large block of land with a front lawn and a verandah that stretched the length of the house. It had a sunroom, which doubled as Diana's bedroom, where we played our favourite game, 'The Busy Bee Club'. This sunroom was our secret hideout, an imaginary place where we could tell stories and live in a world of make-believe. The toilet was what was commonly known as an outhouse and was positioned at the end of a long path through the overgrown backyard. It was made from dilapidated green weatherboard planks, with a corrugated-iron roof that leaked when it rained. The outhouse was not hooked up to the electricity, so there was no light, which made it a scary venture in the dark. We would never go alone at night and would wait until we all needed to use the toilet, then shuffle outside hand in hand to ward off any boogie men or spiders we might encounter along the way. The winters were the worst: we would stand outside the toilet door in our dressing gowns, shivering, waiting for our turn, then peeing as fast as we could so we could scurry back to bed.

I wish I could say that house brought back happy memories, but the four years we lived there were full of pain. It was during this time that I came to believe happy times were for other families, not ours. Dad worked five days a week drycleaning and Mum worked in the drycleaners' pickup agency to bring in a little extra money. We all had to share the responsibility of preparing dinner while Mum was at work, so when we got home from school we had to peel the potatoes and put the meat on, set the table and bring in the washing. Monday to Friday passed easily enough; it was the weekends that would send our family into turmoil.

Dad would come home on a Friday afternoon and start on his first flagon of beer, followed by another and another, before moving on to a flagon of sherry. We would sit in the living room, huddled up on the couch, waiting for his call. We cringed when we heard him scream out, 'Stellaaaaaaaa,' or 'Dianaaaaaaaa,' or 'Rebeccaaaaaaa.' He would very rarely call the boys. Dad had an old record player and he would listen to the same songs over and over again, songs like 'Girl on a Swing', 'The Carnival Is Over', and bands such as The Beatles, Jerry and the Pacemakers, and The Seekers, to name a few. When we were summoned we would have to make our way down the hallway to the back of the house where Dad would sit for hours on end, drinking and playing his music. We would sit there with him, sometimes for an hour, just listening in silence. I was luckier than my sister Diana—Dad seemed to favour her and would call for her more often.

By the time Mum put us to bed, Dad would be very drunk. I don't know how she stayed so calm when she knew what was coming. After tucking us in tight, she would stand in the doorway, singing us lullabies to help us sleep. My favourites were 'Kiss me Goodnight, Sergeant Major' and 'God Bless'. 'God Bless' was a song Mum made up for us; it went like this: 'God Bless Mummy, God bless Daddy, God bless Diana too. God bless Patrick, God bless Michael, God bless Teresa, Stella and Rebecca too. God bless all the boys and girls and mummies and daddies too, and God bless everyone, dear Lord, and make us good for you.' I don't know how Mum could sing those words with such conviction every night before she was about to be beaten, but she had a belief in God that seemed to be unshakable.

As she left the room she would leave the door open slightly because we were afraid of the dark. I remember curling up in the foetal position, holding my hands over my ears to block out the yelling and crying that was to come. Sure enough it wouldn't be long before Dad began shouting at Mum. This would be followed by Mum's screams for help as she was dragged about the house by her hair. I was very fearful and scared for Mum, but couldn't do anything to help. I felt powerless to change anything and never spoke to my mum about it when I was a child. I was very afraid of men and the power they had over women.

By the time I was eleven my eldest brother Michael left home to join the army. He was also very fearful of Dad. Shortly afterwards my sister Teresa left to get married at sixteen, after she and Dad had had a huge fight. I remember that night clearly. It was a Saturday and Teresa had been out with her boyfriend. When she arrived home, my father, as usual, was drunk in the kitchen, his music blaring. After so many years of living under Dad's tyranny, Teresa lost it. 'I can't stand this music, I hate it, and I hate being here!' she screamed.

'All right then!' screamed Dad right back. 'You hate this music, so I'll burn it all.' And with that, he began to cart all of his favourite albums out into the backyard. He called to us kids, 'Get out of bed, we're having a bonfire.' One by one we crawled out of bed and made our way to the yard, where we found Dad standing over a huge fire he had built, flames billowing into the night sky. He was so angry he heaped record after record onto the pyre.

It wasn't long before we heard the sounds of sirens—the neighbours had called the fire brigade. There we all were, standing shivering and dazed in our dressing gowns as the firemen doused the flames. It was just another Saturday night in the Gibney household.

That was not the first time the fire brigade had been called to our house. Some months earlier we had been woken in the early hours of the morning by a neighbour banging on our front door and shouting, 'Get out! Get out! Fire! Fire!' Mum ran through the house, rousing us all from our beds. Outside, we could hear the sound of sirens drawing closer. There was smoke billowing from the eaves as the kitchen had caught alight some time earlier. We were all safe, but sadly our pet budgies had perished. Toffee Nose and Boris had lived in the kitchen, which was gutted by the fire. The fire chief said we were lucky to be alive. If Dad hadn't shut the kitchen door behind him when he went to bed, the fire would have ripped through the house within minutes, making it impossible for any of us to escape. Dad might have saved us, but he had caused the fire in the first place. He had been drinking and, when he'd gone to bed, had left the kerosene heater on in the kitchen. A draught of wind had swept under the door, blowing the open flame onto the sheepskin rug in front of the heater. Apparently the fire had been smouldering for hours. The heat was so intense that it melted a solid silver cross that hung above the mantelpiece.

Chapter Three

My friend Sarah lived in a huge house at Waimarama Beach, a forty-minute drive from Hastings. I stayed over with her as often as I could, just to get away from my father's drinking. I could never invite her to my house, of course, but she seemed to understand that.

Sarah's house was hexagonal, with a spacious living area in the centre. The bedrooms led off the living room and each had a glass door, so it was almost impossible to sneak out at night without Sarah's parents noticing. We were thirteen years old and keen for excitement so, telling her parents we couldn't sleep because of the light from the living room, we taped an old sheet over the door. We waited until the house was quiet and Sarah's parents were in bed and then we snuck out of the bedroom window and made our way down to the beach. Usually we'd just hang around and share a cigarette. Tonight was going to be different, though.

As we wandered down to the beach, Sarah told me we were meeting up with her new boyfriend and he was bringing a friend for me. When we got to the sand dunes I could see the silhouette of two boys walking towards us. They introduced themselves as John and Anthony. The next thing I knew, Sarah was arm in arm with John and wandering off towards the beach, yelling out to me, 'See ya back here a bit later then.'

I began to feel nervous, alone in the dark with a boy I didn't know, although he was pretty cute, a real surfy type with long golden locks that shone in the moonlight. He grabbed my hand and we headed down to the beach.

'Shall we stop here?' he whispered when we reached the sand.

'Sure, why not?' I answered.

Having never been taught how to say no, I just sat there as he leaned over and began kissing me. I remember thinking, *No!* in my head, but the words wouldn't come out. I was thirteen years old and here I was with a sixteen-year-old boy who was fondling me in places I had not been touched since I was six. I found myself in another situation where a man had power over me and I didn't know how to say no to him.

•

April and I had met at school and become close friends, hanging out together most days. I didn't care for school, maybe because I never felt I was good at anything. I certainly never excelled in any subject, so I looked for every opportunity not to go to school. Having a friend like April made that easy—she hated school too. We would often wag and head off into town for the day.

One day we'd been wandering around the city, looking in the windows at the clothes we couldn't afford, when we spotted one of the most stunning shirts I had ever seen. It was a pale lemon floral print with little cap sleeves and a frilled skirt around the waist.

'Go on, why don't you try it on?' April said.

'Whatever for? I could never afford anything like that.'

'Oh, don't think about that. Let's just go inside and you can try it on for fun,' April said, and walked into the shop.

'What size are you?' she asked, going through the racks.

'An eight or a ten, I think, but I don't really know. I've never bought anything new, so I'm guessing.'

'Here you go, take these.' April handed me three hangers and three shirts and pushed me towards the changing rooms. 'I'll come in with you,' she insisted, opening the cubicle door.

I slipped off the old white T-shirt that was a hand-me-down from Teresa and Diana. The top was gorgeous. It fitted like a glove and I felt so good in it.

'It looks lovely on you,' April said as she began taking another shirt off its hanger.

'What are you doing?' I asked.

'Never mind. Just take that top off and put it back on the hanger,' she said, as she began stuffing the shirt in my bag.

'We can't do that,' I whispered nervously.

'Why not? They won't miss it. Besides, you don't have any nice clothes and you deserve it,' she said, grabbing the two hangers and leaving the third on the floor under the chair.

'But they'll know, I'm sure of it!' I exclaimed. 'And it's stealing. I've never stolen anything in my life!'

'Sssshhhh,' April whispered as she unlocked the cubicle door. 'I'll pop these back on the rack and meet you outside.'

I was used to doing what anyone asked of me, so I did what I was told. I made my way nervously to the front of the shop, all the time waiting for a tap on the shoulder from one of the staff. Surely they would have noticed something. But then I was safely outside and there was April, waiting calmly as though this was nothing out of the ordinary.

We headed towards the bus station at the other end of town. 'See ya tomorrow!' April yelled, running ahead of me to catch her bus. 'Oh, and tell your mum I was given the top and didn't want it, so I gave it to you. You'll be fine, just tell her that. See ya,' and she jumped on the bus.

That was easy for April to say. She often lied to her mum and had stolen before, so I guess it was no big deal to her. But I wasn't used to deceiving anyone, especially my mum, who was scrupulously honest. Feeling slightly sick, I waited anxiously for Mum to arrive home from work. When she walked in the back door, looking exhausted, she asked, 'So how was school today?'

'Oh, it was okay,' I replied. 'Just another boring day. How was your day?'

Mum looked puzzled—she wasn't used to being asked how her day was. 'Fine, dear. Are you all right?'

'Oh yes, I'm great. In fact I'm really happy—April gave me a gorgeous shirt today and I love it. Wanna see it?' I asked.

'In a moment, dear, I just need to get changed.'

'Great! I'll go and get it and bring it in to show you.' I hurried down the hall to my room. I was nervous as I grabbed the top off my bed. I felt my hands beginning to tremble. I slowly walked up to Mum's bedroom door. 'Can I come in?' I called.

'Yes, dear,' she said, and I peered around the door.

'What do you think? Isn't it beautiful?' I held up the top; it really was lovely.

'Oh yes, it's very nice, but why didn't April want it? And where did she get it from? I didn't think she had any money.'

'It was a gift, I think,' I lied.

'Really?' Mum raised her eyebrows. 'Are you sure? Are you telling me the truth?'

My heart sank. I knew my mum and I could tell she

thought something wasn't right. I couldn't look her in the eye, so I looked down at the floor.

'Dear, please tell me the truth.'

Tears filled my eyes and I looked up. 'I'm so sorry, Mum, we didn't go to school today. We went into town and April suggested we try on some clothes and we found this in one of the stores and I fell in love with it. April stuffed it in my bag and told me I deserved to have something new,' I said in a rush.

Mum's expression changed. 'I'm disappointed, Stella. I thought I'd taught you that stealing is wrong?'

'You did, Mum. I'm sorry, I won't do it again. It was April's idea. Do you want me to give it back to her?' I asked.

'No, it wasn't hers to give. You can take it back to the shop you stole it from,' Mum said.

I was really scared now. 'But they'll call the police! Please don't make me!'

'I want you to learn from this, Stella, so I want you to take it back the same way you stole it.'

I was relieved that I wouldn't have to go back to the shop and confess. 'I will,' I promised. 'Tomorrow, after school. Will you come with me?'

Thankfully Mum wasn't working the next day, so we could go together. It was weird, because even though I was sad I wasn't going to keep the top, I felt good that I was doing the right thing.

April wasn't at school the next day. I was relieved, because I wasn't good at standing up for myself and she would probably have told me to tell my mum to go jump. The day seemed to drag and I couldn't concentrate on anything other than what I had to do that afternoon. Was I going to get caught? I was nervous and couldn't wait for the ordeal to be over and done with. At home Mum was ready, waiting for me. 'Are you all right, dear?' she asked when she saw my pinched face.

'I'm okay, just a little nervous.'

'You'll be fine, I'll be with you.' And the funny thing was, I knew that if Mum was by my side, I would be fine.

At the store, Mum followed me to the rack where the tops were and said, 'Now you take these into the dressing room, and you know what to do after that. I will be just outside the cubicle,' she said, handing me two tops identical to the one I had taken.

I was shaking as I pulled the top from my bag. Slowly I began stuffing it up underneath one of the other tops on the hanger, smoothing it out, trying to make it look like there was only one top hanging there. I grabbed both hangers, holding them tight together, and opened the door.

'Now, let's pop them back,' Mum said quietly.

I placed them carefully back on the rack, trying to hide the fact there were now three tops on two hangers. I breathed a sigh of relief when I looked around and saw there were no other customers in the shop, and the shop assistant was busy dressing a mannequin in the window. She hadn't noticed. Even though I would have loved to own that top, it certainly wasn't worth the feelings of guilt I had been carrying the previous two days. I had learned a valuable lesson that day. It was far more important to be the person of integrity that Mum had always taught us to be, rather than someone I wasn't.

•

That same year, I got my first tattoo. I didn't really like tattoos, but all the in-crowd had one and, because I was desperate to be accepted, I thought it would be a good idea if I got one too. I knew Mum wouldn't approve, but I could easily hide it from her. I was going to get tattooed on my left wrist, where it would be hidden by my watch.

So I stayed back after school one afternoon to meet Rangi, one of the Maori girls who was considered the best tattoo artist.

'Hey girl,' she said, coming up behind me. 'You havin' a tat today?'

'Yep, that's me.'

'Okay, sit here and we'll get this done in no time at all.'

I stretched out my arm and Rangi rested it on her school blazer. Then she pulled out the biggest darning needle I had ever seen! Dipping it into an inkwell she had brought from class, she began puncturing my skin with little sharp hammering movements. It hurt at first, as the needle pierced my skin, but I got used to it as she went faster and faster, pricking away until finally it was done, a big black circle on my wrist. It wasn't a pretty tattoo; in fact, it was really ugly. I felt a sense of relief, though. Now I would be accepted by the crowd, I was now one of them. I wasn't really, of course, as I found out soon enough.

It was a Friday night, so shops were open until 9 pm. April and I had been into town, wandering through the streets. It was 9 pm and the shops were closing, so we headed back towards the bus station. The streets were deserted. Hastings wasn't a particularly safe place to be on a Friday night after closing—most sensible people knew that and had gone home hours ago. Of course, my mum thought I was safe at April's house. As we got closer to the bus station, we saw a group of girls walking towards us. There were about five of them, and as we got closer, it was obvious they were looking for trouble.

April whispered, 'Quickly, you go that side and I'll go this side,' and she veered towards the gutter of the footpath. That only left me one option—to walk as close to the shop windows as I could as they passed. I tried to avoid looking them in the eye, but one of the girls started moving towards me. I had nowhere to go, I was cornered.

'Ay, what you looking at girl!' she shouted, spitting on me. Then, without warning, she raised her arm and swung at me, punching me right between the eyes.

I almost passed out with the pain and shock as I tried to regain my balance. It was all over within thirty seconds and they wandered off, laughing. April didn't know what to do. We just kept going towards the bus station.

Why me? I kept thinking. *Why do all these bad things keep happening to me?*

Chapter Four

After the fire we moved to a house across the road from the Hastings racecourse. My brother Patrick was keen on horses, and after spending time with the local jockeys who trained every morning on the course, he decided to become an apprentice jockey. We girls were thrilled and would spend all our spare time across at the track, flirting with the jockeys. Mum worked as a cleaner at the racecourse, and after a race meeting we used to scour the course for tickets that had been thrown away, hoping to find one with a payout, discarded by mistake. We always looked harder if there had been an enquiry into the placings, because people might have thrown their tickets away, thinking they hadn't won anything. Every now and then we would find winning tickets.

It was while we were living in this house that Dad had his first stroke. He was only 44. He had gone to bed early, feeling unwell. Suddenly he called out to Mum: 'Help!' Mum found Dad lying on the bed, unable to move the left side of his body. The left side of his face was drooping. Mum called the ambulance and he was taken to hospital.

Dad wasn't the same after that night. He still got drunk and angry, but he didn't have the strength to hit Mum any more. That didn't always stop him, though. One day he was so enraged he threw an ottoman at her, breaking her arm. I ran towards him, intending to protect Mum, but Dad pushed me to the floor. Just then my brother Michael ran in. He was home for a weekend break. He grabbed Dad by the arm and shoved him to the ground. Michael was nineteen now, and fit after all his army training, and he felt he could stand up to Dad. He was old enough to know he didn't have to watch the abuse any more and be powerless to stop it.

My view of Dad changed a little at this time. It was really sad on the one hand to see him deteriorate physically, but he was less capable of abusing Mum, who would often have to carry him to the bathroom or to bed. She became his carer.

Most of the time, though, it was fun living in this house. Michael taught me to drive in his little green Hillman Imp. It was a cute little car with a long gear stick. I was only fourteen, but I could get my licence at fifteen, so I begged Michael to teach me whenever he was home.

Mum and Dad won a share in the Golden Kiwi lottery. Dad had had a dream in which he won the Golden Kiwi with a syndicate called 'Gobble, Gobble' after the turkeys we kept in our backyard. He started using that name for his syndicate's ticket and it wasn't long before they won! His share of the winnings was four thousand dollars, a lot of money back then.

Mum and Dad bought a new car with the money and gave me and Patrick their old Austin. It was pretty much on its last legs, so we decided to enter it in the Demolition Derby at our local raceway. We painted it black and turned its headlights into eyes. Patrick was going to do the driving. On the night, the flag went down and they were off. The car only made it around the track twice, then Patrick was hit from behind and forced into the car in front, blowing a huge hole in the radiator. It was a shame it was over so quickly, but it was fun nonetheless.

I liked hanging out with Patrick. He was a cool seventeen year old, with long wavy hair, and he used to ride motorbikes, which I loved. He also had some handsome mates, like Brenton. Brenton had been on periodic detention, which was like a kind of probation period, and needed somewhere to stay. He moved into the bigger bedroom with Patrick; Rebecca and Diana moved into the smaller room, and I moved my bed and a small bedside table into the living room. It wasn't long before I started flirting with Brenton; he was cute and older than me and I loved the attention. I always felt good when boys noticed me. It wasn't long before we were an item.

I would do anything he asked, even sneak into his room at night, risking being caught by my parents. I would lie awake, reading, waiting for Mum and Dad to go to bed. Mum was always last to go to bed and she must have been surprised to see me reading so much all of a sudden, but she never commented. When the house was finally dark and there was not a sound to be heard, I would climb out of bed, stuffing my pillow under the covers, and tiptoe up the hallway, slowly turning the handle to Patrick's room, trying not to make any noise. I would creep over to Brenton's bed, trying not to wake my brother, and slide in next to him. The whole time I would lie with half an ear open for any noises, scared Mum or Dad might get up in the middle of the night to go to the toilet—the bathroom was at the other end of the house and they would have to walk through the living room to get there. I was scared of Brenton's reaction if I didn't do what he said. The times I didn't creep into Brenton's bed, he would often react by doing hurtful things to make it obvious. One day, out in the backyard, he began shooting a BB gun at my feet, making me dance. Then, another time, he spun me round and around the kitchen, only to let me go, making me fall into the doorway cutting my face above my eyes.

It was always a relief making it back to the safety of my bed. I thought no one knew, until my older sister Teresa spoke to me. Teresa and I were a lot alike and she seemed to know what was going on without me telling her. 'You don't want to be falling pregnant,' she whispered to me one day, slipping me a packet of contraceptive pills. I started taking the pill the very next day, hiding the packet under a book on my bedside table where I was sure no one would find it.

A few days later, I was sitting on my bed and Mum came into the room. 'I need to speak to you about something,' she said, ushering me towards the bathroom. I followed her and she closed the door behind us. 'What are these?' she asked as she pulled the packet of contraceptive pills from her pocket.

It seemed Rebecca, who was ten at the time, had been riffling through my bedside table, like little sisters do, and, finding the packet, had taken it to Mum. She wasn't to know what the little pills were, she was too young. I was fourteen at that time.

'I'm sorry, Mum. Teresa gave them to me. Please don't be mad at me.'

'Then promise me you will never do it again!' she said and began flushing the pills down the toilet. Mum was disapproving and fearful of how Dad would react. She knew he would react angrily and that she would bear the brunt of his anger.

'I won't, I promise. I'm sorry, please forgive me!' I hated being in Mum's bad books. She was always so kind and gentle and I felt like I had let her down, but how could I tell her what was really going on, that I was being forced to have sex?

'When was your last period?' Mum asked.

'Um, about a month ago, I think,' I replied quietly.

'Well, I think it's wise to have a pregnancy test just in case.' I hadn't really considered the possibility of falling pregnant. I felt ashamed of myself and upset that I had let everybody down. It was as if I could do nothing right.

Mum made a doctor's appointment for the next day. The doctor was softly spoken and friendly, and he asked me to go and pee into a small plastic cup. 'All right, just sit tight and I'll be back soon,' he said when I returned with the sample. They were the longest few minutes of my life. Time seemed to stand still as I said over and over in my mind, *What will I do if I'm pregnant?*

The doctor returned and, looking at the floor, walked slowly back to his desk. He sat down, then looked up at Mum. 'I'm afraid your suspicions are confirmed, Mrs Gibney. Your daughter is pregnant.' I went into a state of shock.

Mum looked at me with tears in her eyes. 'It'll be okay, we'll work something out,' she said, stretching out to take my hand. I held on tight as I fought back the tears. What now?

We arrived home around 6 pm, walking past Dad, who

was in his favourite chair in the kitchen, glass in hand and a flagon of beer on the floor next to him.

'Where have you been?' he asked.

'I'll tell you soon,' Mum said and led me into the living room. She sat down on the lounge, next to Brenton, and said softly, 'Stella is pregnant.'

A look of horror crossed Brenton's face. 'I'm so sorry,' he said, lowering his head into his hands.

'Now I have to tell your father, Stella,' Mum said. 'Just wait here and I'll call you if he wants to see you.'

I was scared. How would Dad react? Mum had been so kind but I was sure Dad would be furious.

'Brenton, come in here!' Dad shouted out from the kitchen.

I followed at a safe distance, not wanting to see Dad's reaction up close.

'Sit here, my man,' he said to Brenton. 'Looks like you need a drink,' and he poured Brenton a glass of beer from his flagon. 'Cheers! Here's to having a baby.'

I could hardly believe my ears, but when Dad was drunk he was always unpredictable. I couldn't tell whether he was being sarcastic or genuinely light-hearted. I had an inkling when he wouldn't speak to me all evening, but when I heard him shouting at Mum that night I knew he was furious and his reaction to Brenton had just been drunken bravado.

The next morning I was sitting on my bed when Mum walked in. 'Your father wants you to have an abortion,' she said sadly. Dad was probably worried about how my pregnancy would reflect on him as a parent, particularly after Teresa had also had a teenage pregnancy. This took precedence over any religious convictions he may have had.

'But I don't believe in abortion, Mum. Can't I just have the baby and adopt it out?'

'I am sorry, dear, I don't believe in abortion either. But your father has said he wants you to have one, so we need to get you to the doctors again.' It had been instilled in us from a very young age that we just had to do what Dad said. We could see the power that Dad had over Mum, over all of us. We were afraid and we just did as we were told.

Back in the early seventies in New Zealand it wasn't easy to get an abortion; women had to appear before a team of doctors who would decide their fate. Mum made an appointment for the next day. We arrived at the clinic and sat nervously waiting to be called. A door opened and a tall, heavy-set man emerged. 'You can come in now,' he said, waving his hand and summoning us into the room. Inside there were five doctors sitting around a huge table.

'Please, sit down,' said the heavy-set man. 'Now, Mrs Gibney, we have discussed your daughter's situation and, after careful consideration, we have decided to decline your request for an abortion. We, as a team of professional doctors, have decided your daughter is fit and healthy and capable of carrying this child to full term.'

Mum looked across at me with a smile. 'Thank you,' she replied.

I was washed with a sense of relief. I will be forever grateful to those doctors for making that decision. They saved the life of my firstborn son, Corey.

I wasn't looking forward to going home to tell Dad the news, but Mum reassured me, said she'd talk to him. I never found out how he reacted because Mum shielded me from it. Dad wouldn't tell me himself because he rarely spoke to me. I was the quiet one, the one without a voice; Diana and Patrick were Dad's favourites and I just seemed to slip under his radar. However, within a few weeks we were moving to Wellington. Mum assured me it was because Dad had found a job as a gardener at the botanical gardens as he could no longer stand up for long periods to work at the drycleaners, but I was convinced he felt I had shamed him by falling pregnant at such a young age. I was fourteen.

Brenton wasn't fazed by the news we were moving. In fact, I was struck by how casual he was saying our goodbyes when we packed up the car to leave. 'Hope it all goes well,' he said as he kissed me on the forehead. 'Maybe I'll come and visit one day.' I think he was relieved he didn't have to take responsibility for the baby. That was the last time I ever saw him.

Chapter Five

We arrived at our new home in the suburb of Wilton, a suburb just north of the city, in Wellington. It was another old house, but I loved the street it was in. It had a reservoir at the end where I could escape for peace and quiet. Dad started work at the botanical gardens, doing a bit of gardening and maintenance work, and Mum got a job at a local fruit market. I had left school at the end of 1974 when I was fourteen. I had never really liked school and in the final term I had sixty half-day absences when I was wagging. Nor did I have a job, so I would go to work with Mum to fill in the day.

Me in Dad's arms, with my brothers, Michael, Patrick, and sisters Diana and Teresa. If only Dad was this happy all the time, Levin, 1961.

Dad and me (aged five) on the back doorstep in Levin, 1965.

Off to my first day of school with my siblings, Fairfield Primary School, Levin, 1955.

Rebecca had star quality written all over her way back then. Me and Rebecca Hastings, 1969.

Sisters ready for a swim in the backyard under the hose. Teresa, Diana, Rebecca and me, Masterton, 1968.

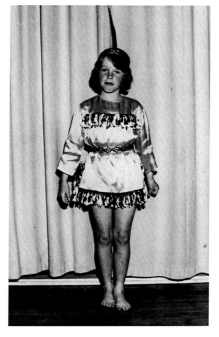

In costume, aged seven, ready for the Maori Culture play, Masterton, 1967.

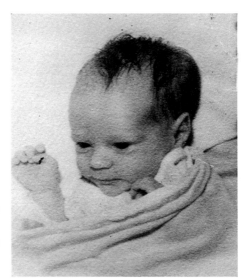

The only photo I had taken of my first-born son, Corey. I carried it with me throughout my life until the day we were reunited, 2 August 1997.

Me aged 19 at a photographic shoot for a modelling course at the Plume Model Agency, Wellington, 1979.

Visiting Patrick in hospital after his brain tumour operation in 1982. Mum, Teresa, Rebecca, Patrick's wife Annie and me.

My wedding day, 25 August 1984, at Wellington, with my sisters Diana and Rebecca as bridesmaids.

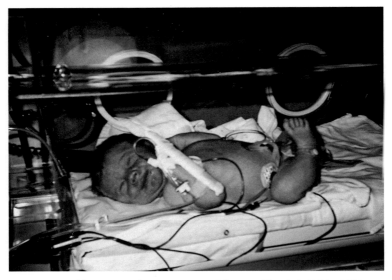

Josh, one day old, in an incubator in ICU at Wellington Hospital, 30 May 1986.

Rebecca, Mum and me, taken after interviewing Mum for an article on her work with Whitcliffe Bible Translators in Darwin, 1990.

One of the privileges of being a celebrity's sister is going to the People's Choice Awards. Photo with Rebecca, Peter O'Brien and Jane Hall.

Happier times with my gorgeous sons before Kieran and I separated. Josh aged 7, Jem aged 5, Springwood, Brisbane, 1994.

Photoshoot for a magazine in Melbourne, circa 1991. Rebecca tells me a joke to make me laugh so the photographer can get the shot! (© Andrew Chapman Photography)

It wasn't long before I met my next boyfriend, Wayne. He was gorgeous, tanned with shoulder-length wavy blond hair. We spent nearly every waking moment with each other. He would come to stay at my house on occasion, but I would mostly stay at his place. Wayne loved cars and enjoyed nothing more than spending his weekends with his head under the bonnet. He taught me all about cars; we replaced spark plugs, did a full service, changed disk brakes. For the first time in my life I was learning how to do something I enjoyed.

Wayne and I had been going out for a few months and I still hadn't told him I was pregnant. My baby bump was still quite small and I wore loose-fitting clothes, so it wasn't obvious. It was something I wanted to keep secret for as long as possible for fear of losing my new love. The day came, however, when I could hide it no longer.

It was a Sunday night and Wayne and I had spent the day together. 'I need to tell you something,' I said as we pulled up outside my house in his car.

'What is it?' he asked, leaning over to hug me.

'Wait,' I said. 'You might not want to be with me after I tell you.'

'Don't be silly,' he said. 'I love you, it can't be that bad.'

'It can!' I cried. 'I'm sorry I didn't tell you earlier. When I was in Hastings just before I moved to Wellington, I was in a relationship with a guy and I fell pregnant to him.'

That was it, my big secret was out. I sat back in the seat, feeling relieved but anxious about his response.

I certainly wasn't expecting what Wayne said next.

'Oh, I thought you were getting a little thick around the middle,' he said, laughing. 'Are you going to keep the baby? It's okay if you are, I'll stay with you. I love you no matter what you decide.'

'I have decided to have my baby adopted.' I couldn't believe it. Here was my prince, the perfect man—handsome; funny, with a cheeky smile; and he loved me—so why didn't I stay with him?

•

It was 9 am on 2 August 1975 when I had my first contraction. I just knew this was it, even though I had never had a contraction before. I was still in bed because it was a Saturday and I didn't have to go to work with Mum. 'Mum!' I cried out. 'I think I'm in labour!'

Mum came into the room and sat on the bed. 'Today's the day,' she said gently.

I was scared, but felt calm knowing I had my mum with me. Two hours later the contractions were coming every twenty minutes. 'I think it's time to go to the hospital,' Mum said and began packing the last few things in my overnight bag. 'I'll call the hospital and let them know you're coming in.'

I was admitted to the maternity ward, where I was put in a gown ready for theatre. Wayne arrived a few minutes after I was admitted, but he was asked to remain in the waiting room. The contractions started coming fast, every four minutes now. 'It hurts, it hurts!' I cried.

Mum tried her best to comfort me, 'It's okay, you'll be fine, it will be over soon.'

I screamed at her, 'You don't know what it's like! Leave me alone!' Looking back, I laugh at that—my mum had given birth to six children, so she of all people knew what labour was like!

The next few minutes were more painful as the doctor examined me. 'She's almost fully dilated so we need to take her to theatre.' Mum wasn't allowed to come with me, so the nurse had to hold my hand as they wheeled me into theatre. There the doctor said, 'I want you to take deep breaths and hold on for as long as you can until I say push.'

I felt the next contraction coming faster and harder than the last one. 'HELP!' I shouted.

'Good girl,' the doctor said calmly. 'I can see the head, now *push*.'

With everything that was in me, I pushed as hard as I could, screaming in pain, feeling like I was about to split in two. Then it was over, just like that, the pain stopped and I felt utter relief.

'It's a wee boy,' the nurse said as I heard my baby's first cries. She wrapped him in a cloth and brought him over to show me. 'I see you've given him the birth name of Chris. He's a beautiful wee thing.'

Just then the door opened and the matron walked in. 'Give him to me,' she said abruptly. 'The girl is not to hold him—this baby is being adopted.' She took my baby from the nurse's arms and left the room, closing the door behind her.

That's it, I thought. *I will never see my baby again.* I curled up on the bed. It was incredibly painful to have my baby wrenched away.

Mum was allowed back in the room to see me. 'How are you doing?' she asked gently. Mum really helped me at that time. We had done up a parcel of booties and a bunny rug as a gift to the new parents and so that something of me would go with the baby to his new life.

'I'm fine now, but I'm sad I couldn't hold Chris. The matron came in and took him away.'

'I'll go and find the doctor and have a word to him,' said Mum. She returned a few minutes later. 'I got to hold him,' she told me. I was upset that she had held him and I hadn't. 'We can go down to the nursery and you can look at him through the glass window.'

The nursery was full of tiny bassinets all lined up in a row. I peered through the window. 'Which one is he?' I asked. Mum pointed. There he was, the cutest little baby I'd ever seen, with fine dark hair and the tiniest face. As we stood there admiring him, the nurse came up behind us and asked, 'Would you like a photo of your baby?'

'Oh please, could I have one? I'd cherish it forever.' Back in those days a photographer would come into the nursery and take instant Polaroid photos. I was so grateful he was there that day. I made a copy for Mum and we both carried that photo with us for the next twenty-two years.

•

It was breakfast time the next morning and I could hear the trolleys coming up the hallway when a nurse popped her head around the curtain. 'Excuse me, Miss Gibney,' she said, 'but we're short-staffed at the moment and I was wondering if you would mind feeding your baby for us.'

I was speechless at first, not knowing whether to laugh with joy or cry with the thought of holding him then having to let him go again. 'I would love that,' I replied, and she returned a few moments later with a little bundle wrapped in a cotton blanket. Holding him close to me, I began feeding him from a bottle of formula the nurse had prepared. He was the most gorgeous baby I had ever seen. I cradled him in my arms, rocking him back and forth.

It went all too quickly, though, and the nurse returned just ten minutes later. 'I'm sorry, but I have to take him back to the nursery now,' she said kindly. I didn't allow myself to think too deeply about the future. There was such a sense of loss and grief within me, and I knew I had to let him go and then try to get on with my life. I kept telling myself that I was doing the best thing for my baby.

'Will he be okay?' I asked.

'Oh yes, the adoptive parents are arriving tomorrow to pick him up.'

My heart sank with the reality of it all. I would never see my baby again. There were so many emotions running through my head and heart. Looking back, I was so young. I told myself I had to move on from this. Even then I had slipped into moving from season to season in my life. Even at that young age I sensed that this was a period in my life that would pass. It was a feeling that resonated with me from that time and which I carried with me. The words 'It's just a season, it will get better' helped to keep me going.

Chapter Six

After I returned home from hospital I was determined to get on with my life. I had been working at the fruit market since we arrived in Wellington but had been looking for another job. I told myself I wouldn't be able to get a decent job because I had left school when I was fourteen and the only work experience I had was bagging fruit. This changed when I made an appointment to visit the dentist. My teeth were in terrible shape, full of decay, and I had a large chip in my front tooth. It was starting to discolour, so I didn't smile a lot, and when I did I covered my mouth. The dentist, Dr Wheeler, was a local who had a small practice not too far from my house.

I was ushered into the surgery by a lovely girl with a big smile. I sat down in the dentist's chair and before I could show what a mess my teeth were in, he said he needed to get a few more details from me. I'd filled in the usual forms, but had left blank those parts I couldn't answer. 'What is your current work phone number?' he asked.

'Oh, I didn't fill that part out because I'm looking for another job,' I told him.

'What are you looking for?' he asked.

I told him I wasn't sure. 'Well, I have a position here if you're interested.'

I couldn't believe my ears! Was he offering me a job? I was sixteen years old, experienced only at fruit bagging! I jumped at the chance. He said the job entailed one week as receptionist, the next week as the dental assistant. I was to start on Monday. I could hardly believe my luck.

I arrived early on Monday morning, keen to impress in my new role. My uniform was similar to a nurse's white coat and I felt very professional in it. Tracy, the young woman with the big smile, showed me around the surgery. She told me that Dr Wheeler had a bit of a temper, but I was used to that, having lived with Dad all these years, so I didn't think much of it.

It was an ordinary Monday morning when I arrived at work for my week as dental assistant. Our first patient had been in several times before; he was a lawyer from the city who took the earliest appointment so as to get into work on time.

'Pass me the clamp,' Dr Wheeler said in a not-so-friendly voice, and as I handed him the clamp, 'Now the pick! Quickly, nurse!'

I began to feel nervous; he hadn't spoken to me like that before. My hand began to tremble a little. As I stretched out to pass him the pick I accidentally dropped it on the patient's chest. 'I'm so sorry,' I said, and looked across at my boss. His face had turned a deep shade of red and he looked as though he was about to explode. All of a sudden he kicked out under the chair, hitting me square in the shins. *Youch!* That hurt. My eyes filled up with tears.

After the patient had left, Dr Wheeler yelled at me, 'Don't ever do that again!' And he walked out of the room, slamming the door behind him.

Tracy was quick to console me. 'He's a mean man, you don't have to put up with that. If he did it to me, I would kick him right back.'

Tracy was a lot stronger than I was, though. I was a pushover, with no courage whatsoever. I always did what I was told and I felt like a failure if I let anyone down. The next few weeks I tried my best to do everything perfectly so I wouldn't annoy Dr Wheeler again. I arrived on time and didn't drop any instruments on the patients. It all seemed to be going smoothly, and apart from the fact he was a grumpy old man, it was a secure job with good pay and it was great working with Tracy.

It was another Monday morning and who else but the lawyer was in the chair. He was in a hurry because he needed to be in the city for a court case. 'Here, quickly, develop these X-rays, the patient is in a hurry,' Dr Wheeler shouted at me.

I grabbed the X-ray plates from him and made my way to the dark room—I'd learnt to develop X-rays as part of the job. I was nervous by now and my hands were shaking. I fumbled trying to open the X-ray's plastic wrapping and the X-ray dropped before I had time to attach it to the clip. OH NO! The X-ray had dropped into the water instead of the developer and was ruined. I was so scared now. I had to face Mr Walker and tell him what I had done. I trudged back to the surgery. 'I am so sorry,' I told him, looking at the floor, 'but I ruined the X-rays.'

'You *what?*' he exploded. 'Come with me.' He grabbed my arm and pulled me into the reception area. 'You stupid girl, stay here and we will deal with this later!' he shouted, then turned and walked swiftly back to the surgery.

I burst into tears. 'He's right. I'm so stupid!' I cried.

'No, you are not,' Tracy exclaimed. 'Don't you dare let him treat you like that. Grab your bag and leave. Go on, take your stuff and go!'

Trying to wipe the tears from my eyes, I grabbed my bag and made a quick exit out the back. As I was making my way up the road to catch the bus home, I heard a voice behind me. 'Wait, don't go!' I swung around to see Dr Wheeler running towards me. 'You can't leave!' he said. 'Come back!' I didn't say anything, but like the good girl I always tried to be, I did what I was told and went back to the surgery. I didn't say anything more about the incident, but I only lasted in the job for another week.

I was trying hard to move on in my life but it seemed as though I was continually living in my past, with men constantly holding power over me.

•

I'm not sure what it was that made me leave a loving relationship and the security of home, but I did. Maybe I was running away from myself, or maybe I was suffering from postnatal depression and didn't know it. Whatever the reason, I found myself moving back to Hastings shortly after I finished at the dental surgery.

It was hard telling Wayne. He and I had become almost inseparable. I was only sixteen and didn't really know what love was. Wayne was kind and caring, but we had more of a friendship than anything else. He took me places and showed me things I had never experienced before. My sister Rebecca was very fond of him too and was really upset the day I told Wayne it was over. Before he arrived she came into my room. 'Stella,' she said, 'please don't break up with Wayne. It will make me sad.'

'I'm sorry, sis, but I have to. I'm going back to Hastings to live.'

Just then Wayne knocked on the front door. Rebecca ran to let him in. We went into my room and I closed the door behind me. It wasn't easy telling him it was over, but I knew it had to be done. After shedding tears and hugging, it was time for Wayne to leave. As we came out of my room Rebecca was in the living room. 'Wait,' she said. 'Don't go yet, Wayne.' She ran to the record player and put on a record. She had picked out a song that she hoped would stop me ending the relationship. It was Chicago's latest hit, 'If You Leave Me Now'. It didn't change my mind; it only made it harder to say goodbye.

•

I was sixteen years old when I moved back to Hastings. Patrick had moved back there too and I loved hanging out with his friends, most of whom rode motorbikes. So I guess it's no great surprise that I ended up engaged to a bikie named Steve just a few short months later.

One night a few of us had been at Steve's place fixing his motorbike when Patrick offered to give it a test drive up the street.

'Okay,' Steve said. 'You can ride it up the street . . .'

Patrick swung his leg up over the bike.

'. . . on one condition,' Steve continued. 'You wear a helmet.'

'I'm only going up the street, I'll be right,' said Patrick.

'No way,' Steve said. 'You ain't going to ride my bike without a helmet.'

We watched as Patrick started up the bike and rode across the lawn. He headed out onto the road and called back, 'She seems to be going fine.' He gave us a huge smile, then wound up the bike and disappeared down the road. It was around six in the evening and the streetlights had just come on as we heard the bike coming back down the street. Patrick was probably travelling at around forty kilometres per hour as he passed in front of the house again. We were all standing watching when suddenly a car appeared out of nowhere and pulled into a driveway right in front of the bike. It was terrifying watching as the motorbike hit the front of the car and Patrick was thrown into the air and across the bonnet. He hit the ground and then spun over and over on the bitumen before finally coming to a halt. He lay motionless as we rushed to his side. I held my breath, trying not to panic at the sight of him. But then he moved, and tried to sit up. He was okay, but very shaken. He had deep gravel rash to his arm where the jacket had been torn with the force of impact, and the helmet he was wearing had a huge crack down the back. Thank God Steve had insisted he wear the helmet—that had saved his life—although some doctors would suspect that this accident was the cause of a brain tumour Patrick was to suffer in later years.

My relationship with Steve ended after a few short months and I found myself moving into a house where I was introduced to marijuana. We would have Sunday sessions sitting around the living room, listening to music and smoking weed. I wasn't happy, though and I knew this was not the way I wanted to spend the rest of my life. Six months later I was living back in Wellington.

Chapter Seven

Christmas Day was always fun at the Gibney household in the later years. When Dad wasn't drinking he was kind, funny and caring. We would catch occasional glimpses of this side of him. After breakfast, Mum, Diana, Patrick, Rebecca and I would all scramble into the car and drive the streets looking for anyone who was alone so we could invite them back for Christmas lunch. One Christmas, outside the local pie shop we spotted a handsome young sailor dressed in a white uniform with a white cap. We pulled up alongside him and excitedly jumped out of the car. 'Hello,' said Mum. 'I'm Shirley, and these are my children. What are you doing alone on Christmas Day?'

'I'm Greg,' he replied with the cutest American accent. 'I'm a sailor on the ice breaker, the *Polar Star*. We docked here last night on our way to the Antarctic and we leave tomorrow morning.'

'Well, if you're not doing anything, we'd love you to join us for Christmas lunch,' Mum said.

Greg seemed taken aback. 'That's very kind of you, but why would you invite a stranger back to your home?' he asked.

We told him that we didn't like the thought of anyone being alone on Christmas Day, which seemed to reassure him that we weren't axe murderers because he replied, 'That would be lovely,' and tossed his half-eaten pie in the bin.

We all piled back into the car, giving Greg the front seat. The house we were renting at the time was quite old and dilapidated. Mould was growing in the bedrooms because the house was set back against a hill and never saw the sun. I hoped Greg wouldn't be disappointed. When we arrived home us girls helped Mum in the kitchen, while Dad, Patrick and Greg sat in the living room sharing stories. During lunch Greg told us tales of the missions he had been on and the places he had visited. By the end of the day I was totally mesmerised by him. When it was time to leave Greg said, 'I had fun. It was a lovely meal and you have a lovely family, Mrs Gibney, and to thank you I would love to give you a guided tour of the ship when we get to the wharf.' I was beside myself with excitement and scrambled to beat Diana and Rebecca into the back seat of the car.

Aboard the *Polar Star* there were sailors everywhere. I was in heaven! And because Mum had wanted to get home to start dinner and hadn't wanted to leave Rebecca on board, it was just Diana and me. Greg led us down a small flight of stairs to a narrow hallway with rooms off to both sides. These were the cabins, where the sailors slept for the sixty days and nights they were at sea. They were tiny, with a single bed against the wall, a small desk and a bedside table.

'Who's in the cabin opposite you?' I asked.

'Oh, that's Tom, we're good mates. He's around somewhere. If you wait here I'll see if I can find him.'

I felt my knees go weak when Tom appeared; he was even more handsome than Greg, with beautiful blue eyes and a cheeky smile. Greg introduced us and Tom asked whether I'd like to see the rest of the ship with him. I nodded and he grabbed my hand and led me up to the top deck. I couldn't believe my luck, that a man as handsome as Tom would be interested in me. I mean, I didn't feel attractive, in fact I didn't even like myself, but he didn't know that. He was in uniform, and in a fantasy world he was a knight in shining armour.

We wandered around the ship a while, then Tom asked, 'Would you like to come back to my cabin?'

'Sure, just for a little while.' There I was again, unable to say no, particularly to a man. Maybe it was because I felt men had power over me.

I don't remember how long I was in Tom's cabin, but I do know that all I wanted was to be held, to feel loved for a short while. Eventually I had to leave or Diana would go home without me. I didn't want to go; I wanted to stay all night in his arms. Holding back the tears, I leaned forward and kissed him goodbye. 'Can I come back tomorrow to wave you off?' I asked.

'Sure,' Tom said. 'The ship is leaving at nine, so if you get to the wharf by eight-thirty I'll come down and meet you for half an hour.'

I cried myself to sleep that night. I wanted to be with Tom, but he was leaving. By morning I looked a wreck: my eyes were puffy from crying and they had dark circles around them from lack of sleep.

Tom represented a more glamorous and exciting kind of life, and he was very handsome.

Diana and I arrived at the wharf on time and, to my amazement, Tom and Greg were waiting for us at the bottom of the gangplank. In his freshly starched uniform and sailor's hat, Tom looked even more handsome than he had last night. I ran into his arms and hugged him tight. 'I'll miss you,' I whispered in his ear.

'I'll miss you too,' he replied, kissing me on the cheek. I wanted this moment to last forever, it felt so good being in his arms, but the ship's siren blasted into the morning air to let the sailors know it was time to board the ship. This was goodbye, as he let go of me, kissing me one final time.

'Wait! Do you mind if I take a photo?' came a voice behind us. We turned around to see a man with a camera walking towards us. 'I'm from the *Evening Post* and we're looking to put a few photos in the paper about the *Polar Star*,' he said.

Tom and I hugged tightly as he took the shot. That was the final hug and the last I saw of Tom. I was sad for days, knowing I would never see him again. It sounds silly—I mean, I had only known him for a few hours, so why did I feel so sad?

•

I was nineteen when I met Liam. He was a rugged-looking bloke with a gaunt face and a moustache and wavy blond hair. Before long we were living together in a one-bedroom flat in Wellington. I didn't know much about him except that he had just got out of Long Bay jail in Australia, having been convicted for importing drugs. He had a history of drug dealing and was a heroin addict, although I wasn't aware of that for a number of months. When he finally admitted to it, he promised he would come clean and he enrolled at a methadone clinic. Our visits to the clinic became quite frequent as Liam would often take his weekend supply in one hit then have withdrawal symptoms for the next few days and need more methadone to top up his system. Here I was again, on another roller-coaster ride, not knowing where it would take me but feeling lucky to have someone to love me. I had never known anyone who was into hard drugs like heroin.

Liam was an apprentice architectural draftsman and attended night school. One Thursday he didn't come home after night school. It was 10 pm and I was panicking, ringing every hospital trying to find out if he had been admitted anywhere. I called Mum and she came over to keep me company. Around 11.30 pm he walked in the front door. I was so relieved to see him I didn't react when he told me he hadn't been to night school but had been in a back alley in the city, shooting up.

'How did you manage to pay for it?' I asked, knowing he didn't have any money.

'I'm sorry,' he confessed, 'but I sold your car.' At first I was devastated, but I was also relieved that he was okay. Whenever he was out at night I would worry terribly that something awful would happen to him.

My car was not the only thing Liam sold for his addiction. My sister Diana had lent us a sewing machine, which he sold, and my brother-in-law's leather jacket went missing, never to be seen again. Liam was obviously being deceitful, and when I cleaned the house I found screwed-up pieces of foil in his shoes and bent spoons in his drawers. Was he really trying to stop or was I too trusting?

It was quite exciting being with Liam and it made me feel good to think that I could look after him and 'rescue' him.

We had been together for a little over a year when my whole world was shaken by a terrifying event. I was working at Budget Rent-a-car in Wellington as an assistant manager. The manager Bill believed in me and gave me the sense that I was valued. He helped me to feel good about myself. It had been a busy week and I had been on duty every day. It was my last shift and I was to meet a midnight flight from the airport to deliver a car. At 11.30 pm I called in to the office to collect the car. Liam was with me, as he had to pick me up after I'd dropped the car at the airport. We pulled into the office car park and I noticed a dim light on at the back of the shop. It was the cafeteria light and I thought I had left it on. Not thinking anything of it, I said to Liam, 'I should go in and turn the light off.' He asked whether I wanted him to come with me and I laughingly said, 'Yeah, there might be a boogeyman in there.'

I unlocked the front door and swung past the counter, turning into the tiny office which led to the back door. It was quite dark but there was enough light to see where we were going. I heard a noise and turned to Liam and said, 'Shhh, you might wake the boogeyman.' My heart froze when a deep, husky voice shouted, 'Be quiet!' I turned around. There was a large, thickset man standing behind me, a mutton-cloth mask over his head. All I could see were tiny eyes glaring at me through holes cut in the cloth.

The man pushed Liam to the floor and began tying him up with a long rope. I was too scared to move. 'Now you get over there and open that safe!' he hissed at me.

My lips were trembling as I said in a panic, 'I'm not sure of the combination.' Of course I knew the combination, but in that instant I froze, not knowing what to say.

He grabbed my arm and raised a huge metal bar over my head. 'You bloody better!' he screamed.

The safe was located under the floor behind the counter. I was so terrified, I was shaking so much and my mind was in a whirl trying to remember the combination. I prayed, *God, if you're there, please help me unlock this safe. Please help me!* Somehow in the dark I managed to get the combination right to unlock the safe.

'That's a good girl. Now you get over there and lie on the floor and you won't get hurt.' The intruder tied me up face down alongside Liam and began rummaging through the contents of the safe, shoving travellers cheques and cash into a bank bag. When he was done, he grabbed the telephone cables that were attached to the phone box on the wall and wrenched them out, then stormed into the other office, ripping the phone lines from the wall in there too.

Any means of communication with the outside world was gone. What was he going to do next? Was he going to kill us? I tried not to move, or even to breathe. In my mind I prayed over and over, *If you're there, God, please save us.*

The man walked out of the back door and into the huge garage that was attached to the office. This was where all the rental cars were stored. I heard an engine start up and the creak of the garage doors opening. There was a screech of tyres as the car sped onto the street.

I gave a huge sigh of relief—he was leaving. What I didn't know was whether or not he was coming back. The thought terrified me. Still shaking, I managed to unhook my feet from the rope and started to undo the ties around my wrists. It seemed to be taking forever; all I wanted was for someone to help us. Finally I was free. I undid the rope around Liam's feet, but the knots around his hands were too tight.

'Quick,' I said. 'We have to get someone to call the police right now in case he comes back.' I ran screaming out into the middle of the street, Liam behind me, his wrists still bound. Several cars drove straight past us as I cried, 'Help! Please stop!'

Finally a taxi stopped, then radioed the police, and within minutes there were several police cars on the scene. Still terrified and shaking, we were put in a police car and escorted to the station for questioning.

When we arrived, Liam and I were separated. I was questioned for two hours and it wasn't until three in the morning that we were released and free to go home. Straightaway I called Mum to ask whether we could stay the night with her. I didn't want to go back to the flat. As we walked in the back door Mum was standing there with her arms outstretched. 'You poor girl,' she said, holding me tight. I was still shaking, but I felt safe at home with Mum. I didn't sleep a wink that night. Every time I closed my eyes I relived the ordeal over and over. This was to continue for some years to come. I didn't like the dark, so I would always have a dim light on somewhere in the house. It took many many years for me to stop looking behind me and feeling unsafe.

The next morning we had to meet the investigating officers at the rental office. When we arrived, there were several police cars in the courtyard, a police officer with a sniffer dog on the roof, another taking photos of the crime scene and two standing in the doorway, waiting to meet us. I was nervous enough as I walked in the front door, but all of a sudden the fear I'd felt last night returned and engulfed me. I began shaking uncontrollably.

At that moment my manager, Bill, arrived. 'Are you okay?' he asked.

'I'm okay, Bill. I'm so sorry.' Somehow I felt as though it was my fault.

I managed to hold myself together long enough to talk the police through the events of the previous night. It appeared over twelve thousand dollars had been stolen. I felt sick. 'I'm so sorry, Bill,' I said again.

'It's not your fault,' he said reassuringly. 'Besides, we're insured for this sort of thing. I think you should take some time off, give yourself space to get over what's happened.' Bill was a great boss and he could see how shaken I was.

'Oh Bill, I don't think I could work here ever again. I'm just too scared now. What if it happens again?' I knew with absolute certainty that I couldn't stay in that office by myself. I couldn't even return to the flat. I was convinced Liam wouldn't be able to protect me should anything else happen and I was afraid to be alone with him at night because he hadn't kept me safe.

We stayed at Mum's for the next couple of nights, trying to decide what to do next. I wanted to get away, to leave town for a few days. Someone had told me of a place called the Portage Hotel that was located in the beautiful Marlborough Sounds. It was supposed to be quiet and peaceful and that was just what I needed.

•

Liam and I took the ferry from Picton and chugged across the Sounds. When the ferry pulled up to the wharf at the Portage Hotel, a tanned, weather-beaten man was waiting for us in front of an old rusty yellow bus. He drove us up the dirt track that wound around the hilltop. The track was full of potholes and quite precarious, but we made it safely to the other side. There, in the middle of nowhere, was a quaint little hotel with the words *Welcome to the Portage Hotel* etched on a plank of wood hanging above the entrance. The sun was shining and as I stepped off the bus I felt enveloped by a sense of calm.

We settled into our small chalet. It was surrounded by trees, and felt so quiet and peaceful. We unpacked the few things we had brought with us and made our way back to the hotel for a drink. We sat on a huge wooden deck overlooking spectacular rolling greens hills on one side and the crystal-clear waters of the Marlborough Sounds on the other side. The view was breathtakingly beautiful.

We got chatting to the owners, Bob and Nancy, and the next two and a half hours flew by. We told them of the robbery and our need to get away, and they shared with us their problems with the hotel staff.

'What are your plans from here?' Bob asked eventually.

'I wish I knew,' I said with a small smile.

'Well, we're looking for a barman and waitress and we'd love you to come and work for us.'

I looked at Liam with wide eyes. 'What do you think? I would love that.'

'Sounds good to me,' said Liam.

'That's settled then. You can start next week if you like.'

I was excited and relieved at the same time. I was going to love it here. It was the perfect new beginning I was looking for.

Chapter Eight

My role at the Portage Hotel varied from housemaid to waitress. At 7 am I would make my way to the kitchen to help set up for breakfast, wait tables and clear up. I would finish the restaurant duties by 9 am, then make my way to the rooms and chalets and start cleaning and making beds. By mid-morning I was back in the restaurant preparing for lunch. When lunch was over, I had a few hours off before starting again in the restaurant for dinner, then finishing up around ten, depending on how many people were staying.

For the first week the hotel had few guests, which meant there weren't many beds to make and only a few people to serve in the restaurant. On the third day I decided to go for a walk by myself, which was unusual for me, but somehow I felt I needed it. I wandered up over the hill and, on the other side, discovered a most beautiful sight. A small, secluded sandy beach overlooked the blue waters of the Sounds, surrounded by those beautiful rolling green hills. As I made my way down to the water's edge, I felt free, as though I was the only person on earth. I sat on the sand and looked out to sea for the next hour, soaking up the solitude and serenity. For the first time in a long while it felt good to be alive.

The next day, when I had finished clearing up after lunch, I couldn't wait to return to my special place. This time I wanted to take a pad and pen, in case I felt inspired to write. I really don't know why, because I had never written anything in my life, but somehow in this place I felt truly myself. The beach was even more beautiful than I remembered as I nestled in the warm sand. Looking out to sea, I felt peace washing over me. I picked up my pen and began to write; it seemed the natural thing to do.

The clouds are thick, the day is warm,
I hear a bird cry, the sound has faded now,
The water is still, it breaks, a tiny fish has surfaced.
The wasps are flying low, they smell the fish,
they sense movement and are gone.
Tiny shells are washed up on the beach
drying and cracking in the heat.

The leaves on the trees are blooming
in an atmosphere of freedom,
knowing they can come to no harm
I smell the freshness in the air,
There is silence, I taste salt upon my lips.

It felt so good to write. Unbeknown to me, this was the beginning of a thirty-year journey of writing that would help guide me through the seasons of my life.

Everything seemed perfect during those first few weeks. I had a loving partner; we lived in an idyllic location; we had great jobs with awesome managers. Life couldn't get any better.

The weeks passed quickly and before long the peak season was almost upon us. It was the time of year when fishing groups descended on the hotel. The rooms and chalets were filled with men in their forties coming away for a weekend of fishing and drinking with the boys. 'They go out fishing early in the morning,' Nancy had warned me, 'then drink all day on the boat and come back to the hotel, have a feed and stay up in the bar drinking throughout the night. Liam will have a few late nights with these guys. They're harmless enough but they can get quite rowdy.'

One morning, as I was setting up for breakfast, Nancy walked into the dining room. 'Stella, we have thirty for breakfast this morning, so we'll need to set more tables,' she said, handing me a pile of napkins. By 7.30 am, the tiny restaurant was overflowing with middle-aged men clad in dirty jeans and checked shirts, all talking over the top of each other and claiming to be the one who would catch the biggest fish. It was hectic and I didn't stop until the last man had left the restaurant. 'See ya later, darl. Wish me luck with the big catch,' he grinned.

I had my work cut out for me that day as I made my way around every hotel room and chalet on the property, making beds, cleaning toilets and taking out empty beer bottles. Thankfully the fishing party wasn't around at lunchtime, but at dinner the restaurant was full of men, most of whom were drunk. The smell of fish permeated everything. The men were becoming loud and obnoxious, swearing and slinging off at each other. I was relieved when dinner was over. There was a huge mess but at least it was quiet.

It was my nightly ritual, after my shift was over, to make my way to the bar for a quiet drink with Liam. Tonight in the bar it was raucous. The fishermen had decided to stay up for a few more drinks and were in the bar skolling shots. I really didn't want to deal with them again, but I was afraid to go home alone with so many drunk men about, so I took a deep breath, stuck a false smile on my face and walked right up to the bar where Liam was chatting away to one of the fishermen.

I spent the next couple of hours trying to stay awake during the drunken conversations and dirty jokes.

'You should really go home,' Liam said gently. 'You look exhausted. I could be here for another couple of hours yet.'

My heart sank, I knew he was right but I didn't want to go home alone. It had been six weeks since the robbery and I thought I was getting over the trauma of it, but I hadn't yet been tested like this. *I can do this*, I thought, grabbing a glass of wine for courage. I blew Liam a kiss and made my way out of the bar.

Our chalet was a short walk up the dirt track, just out of sight of the hotel, so I didn't have far to go by myself. It had been overcast all day, and now the moon was hidden behind the clouds. It seemed very dark. I had only walked a few steps when I heard a noise in the bushes. My heart began to race. There must be someone hiding, waiting to jump out at me. I picked up my pace until I was almost running. Fear gripped me, that same fear from the robbery. Shaking and looking over my shoulder every few seconds, I finally made it to the chalet.

I didn't know whether to go inside. Maybe someone was waiting for me in there. What if one of the fishermen was hiding under the bed, ready to ambush me? We never locked the door to the chalet because there was no need: the hotel rarely had more than two dozen guests at any one time and usually these were families.

I slowly turned the handle and pushed the door open, turning on the light as quickly as I could. The chalet was small, so there weren't many places to hide. Still, I didn't close the door behind me in case I needed a quick escape. I bent down to look under the bed. There was no one there. But what about the bathroom? Someone could be hiding behind the shower curtain. I checked: no one. So why was I still convinced there could be an intruder in my room?

Still afraid, I closed the front door and sat on the end of the bed. How could I sleep when there might be someone out there spying on me? The curtains were too small for the window; someone could easily look in and see I was alone. By now I had convinced myself that one of the fishermen was lurking about in the bushes, waiting for me to go to bed before he burst in.

I lay awake for over an hour, jumping at every sound. At around 3.30 am I heard footsteps. My heart began to pound again. Was it Liam or was someone else out there? I froze as I heard the handle of the door turn. Liam's face appeared.

'What are you still doing awake?' he whispered.

'I couldn't sleep. I was scared there was someone out there.'

'Oh, you silly thing, you need to go to sleep, you have to be up in three hours.' He leaned across the bed and kissed me on the forehead.

Almost straightaway I fell into an exhausted sleep, only to hear the alarm clock at 6.30 am.

I was in the restaurant by seven, setting tables for breakfast, another busy day ahead. I was relieved that it was Sunday and the fishermen were checking out that afternoon. I thought things would return to normal. But after the lunch shift ended I realised I didn't want to go down to my favourite place. Somehow it seemed too lonely and isolated. My desire for solitude had been replaced by a horrible fear of being by myself. Now I was afraid, nothing could change that. It was coming into the busy season and the hotel would be jam-packed over the coming weeks. I knew Liam would be working late most every night in the bar, which would mean I would have to go home alone. The thought scared me. Our idyllic life had ended and I didn't want to be here any more. I made the decision to tell Liam after dinner. If he didn't want to go, then I would leave anyway.

Chapter Nine

Christchurch was a lovely city and I felt good about beginning a new life here. Liam had been very understanding about my need to leave the Portage Hotel; he just wanted me to be happy. I was reluctant to return to Wellington, so the other alternative was Christchurch where Liam had grown up.

Although Liam and I had been together for a long time I still didn't feel safe with him. Perhaps this was because he'd been with me the night of the robbery and hadn't been able to protect me, or maybe it was because I still didn't know if I could trust him not to start taking drugs again. Despite this, I was determined to give it my all to make the relationship work.

We found a gorgeous little house to rent, close to the city. It was a deceased estate and was being rented fully furnished. We were given the option to purchase the furniture by paying a little extra rent each week. I was thrilled. The pieces were antique and had been kept in good condition; besides, we didn't have a stick of furniture to our name—we had sold it all when we'd moved to Portage.

I began work as a trainee manager at the Budget depot. Liam went back to being an architectural draftsman and returned to techincal college to finish his course. We made friends quickly and had a busy social life. Our lives were back to normal and I started to feel at home.

It was Friday night and we were heading out for a Fleetwood Mac concert when we realised we had left the keys to the house inside. The house had small windows above the main windows, and fortunately we had left one open. Liam climbed inside, grabbed the key and we headed off. We had a great night and were both on a high when we pulled into our street. As we got out of the car I realised I could see right into our house—every light in the place was on. *Oh no, here we go again,* I thought.

'You didn't turn on any lights when you went in to get the key, did you?' I asked Liam, knowing he hadn't but hoping he would say yes and still the fear that was beginning to rise in my chest.

'No, it was still quite light when we left,' Liam replied, heading off up the driveway.

My heart was pounding. What were we going to find inside? Maybe the intruders were still in there. 'No! Liam, stop! We need to call the police!' I yelled as he reached the front door.

The door was closed but the glass panel had been smashed and there was glass on the porch. 'Don't go in there, Liam. We need to call the police.'

We got into the car and drove to the nearest telephone booth. I scrambled out of the car with him. I didn't want to be alone, not for a moment.

Liam had been on the phone for less than a minute when he started to smile. 'Oh, is that right? Okay, I get it now. Thanks very much,' he said as he hung up.

'How can you smile at a time like this? It's almost two in the morning and someone has just broken into our house,' I cried.

'You know how I climbed in the window to get the key before we went to the concert? Yeah, well, a neighbour called the police saying they'd witnessed a break-in and it was the police who broke into our house to check.' Apparently they had left us a note explaining that inside.

I didn't find it funny at all. I was terrified again and it brought back all the fears I had lived with in Wellington and Portage. They had followed me here to Christchurch.

I couldn't sleep that night. Even though I knew it was only the police who had broken in, I still felt afraid: someone had been in the house and it no longer felt safe. It's hard to explain, but that one night of the robbery had changed everything for me. I couldn't ignore the fact that I didn't feel safe with Liam, as nonsensical as that was. Each night I lay in bed, terrified that someone would break in.

•

Only a matter of days later I received a phone call from Bill, my old boss in Wellington. Apparently I had rented a car to a known drug runner (he was unknown to me, of course). He had been pulled up and drugs had been found in the car. I was the only one who could identify him as the person who had signed for the car. I was being summoned to court and the papers were in the mail.

I decided I would use this as an opportunity to stay with my parents for a few days. It was so good to see Mum's smiling face. I had forgotten how secure I felt around her. She gave me a sense of calm when everything else around me seemed a mess. Things seemed calmer for Mum now.

I didn't sleep the night before the hearing. I was anxious about the repercussions of being the only witness. The drug runner might have mates out there who would hunt me down if I helped get him convicted.

In the witness box the judge asked me, 'Now, Miss Gibney, could you please identify the man you rented the car to. Is he in the courtroom today?'

'Yes, Your Honour, he's over there,' I said, pointing a shaking finger towards the accused. He was a heavy-set man with tattoos down both arms and a tattoo of a skull on his neck. He looked intimidating and I assumed he had his friends in the courtroom as the gallery was full of men of similar appearance.

By midday the case was over and the accused had been found guilty and sentenced to two years' imprisonment. I was terrified to leave the courthouse, though, thinking the men would be waiting for me outside, or would follow me home. I was glad Mum had come with me. She reassured me it was all going to be okay, and I believed her.

I fell into a deep sleep that night and woke up feeling refreshed in a way I hadn't felt in a long time. I decided that I'd make the most of the day and call up a few friends. For some reason I thought of Mark, the man who had broken my heart a few years earlier. Mark was a very handsome guy, the type of guy I would have loved to have been with, but I knew he wouldn't be interested in a girl like me. The night I met him my girlfriend and I were at a wine bar and I was being harassed by a drunken bloke who was trying to persuade me to dance with him. 'Leave her alone,' came a voice out of the blue. I turned around and there was a gorgeous man with thick dark hair and brilliant blue eyes. 'Are you okay?' he asked once the man had slouched off. He introduced himself and joined my girlfriend and me for a drink, then said he needed to head home because he was getting up early to go four-wheel driving. Wow, not only was he a knight in shining armour but he was out in the world doing stuff, not simply drinking himself silly like most of the men I knew.

As he got up to leave, he asked if I would like to go out four-wheel driving the following weekend. I was ecstatic as I handed him my address and phone number. That week couldn't go quickly enough for me. When Saturday finally arrived, I hovered around the phone, hoping each time it rang that I would hear Mark's voice on the other end. It was a long day of waiting. Finally he rang at 6 pm, apologising and asking whether I was free the next day. We drove around the Wellington bays, and it was so nice to be with someone who seemed interested in me. I didn't see myself as attractive and couldn't receive love from anyone. I didn't believe that anything good would last. When we got home, he leaned over to kiss me goodbye. I didn't want to let him get away, so I made every attempt to seduce him. Surely if I had sex with him he would want me—that was all men were interested in me for anyway, right?

The next weekend I anxiously waited for his call—he'd said he would pick me up at midday on Saturday but call me first. I spent the morning getting ready, trying on six outfits before deciding on the right one, and doing my hair and makeup, hoping to make myself look beautiful, even though I felt anything but beautiful on the inside. The clock ticked past midday as I stood staring out the window. The phone hadn't rung and there was no sign of him. That afternoon I stared out of the front window, hoping to see his car pull up at any moment. He didn't call and he didn't turn up either. By 9 pm I was in my room crying myself to sleep. What was it about me that men couldn't love? Maybe if I hadn't seduced him he would have kept our date, or perhaps he thought I was no good and wasn't worth pursuing.

I did see Mark again but many months later. It was at the same wine bar and I was with Liam. We had been together for a few months. Liam was at the bar. Mark smiled across the room and made his way to our table. He looked as handsome as I remembered. He said how nice it was to see me and how sorry he was for not getting back to me. I explained to him I was with Liam now and we were happy. He had heard on the grapevine that Liam was involved in drugs and had been in Long Bay jail, so he was surprised I was with him. As Liam made his way back to the table, Mark leaned over and whispered in my ear, 'You deserve better than that.' Those words stuck with me for years.

Maybe being back in Wellington brought back all those memories, or perhaps I was trying to revisit the past in the few days I was there. Whatever the reason, I decided to call Mark to find out where he was and what he was doing. To my amazement, he was still listed in the phone book at the same address and number I had for him. Picking up the phone, I nervously began dialling, wondering what on earth I was going to say if he answered.

It began to ring, three times, then four. Should I hang up? Then he answered. 'Hello?'

It was him, I knew it. 'Hello,' I said with a shaky voice. 'It's Stella, remember me?'

'Of course I remember. How you are? Where are you living now?'

I told him Liam and I had moved to Christchurch. He was surprised to hear I was still with Liam; he didn't think he was right for me and said I should leave him and do something with my life.

'What do you suggest? I wouldn't know where to start!'

Mark's idea was that I should work in the ski fields; it was coming into winter and there would be jobs available for the season. We chatted for ages; it was so good to talk to him, he seemed so together and I respected his advice. I knew he cared about me and that was important to me. I got off the phone and, without even thinking, straightaway called all of the ski fields in NZ, asking if they had any jobs available. I was up to my old tricks—acting now, thinking later! After three calls I had a job as a child minder and was expected to start in a week.

What on earth am I doing? I thought when I hung up the phone, but I didn't know the answer to that question. All I knew was I had been fearful ever since the robbery and that had made me question everything in my life, including how I felt about Liam. Was I with him because I felt sorry for him? Or did I truly love him? I wasn't sure what love was anyway. I didn't know how to recognise it. There had been no real role models for loving relationships in my life.

Maybe I needed to take a break from the relationship, to get away for a while.

I couldn't sleep that night, so many thoughts were running through my head. How I was going to tell Liam? What would my life look like without him? I decided I couldn't think about that now, I just needed to get on the plane to Christchurch tomorrow, pack up my stuff and get to the ski fields to start my new job.

I landed in Christchurch at 4.15 pm and decided to book a standby flight that evening. If I was going to leave, I needed to do it tonight or I might change my mind. I went straight to the airline counter and put my name down for a flight leaving at 8.30 pm. I decided to drive directly to Liam's work and tell him my plans. I found him sitting at his desk, working on a draft design for a house.

He was startled by my unexpected arrival but he gave me a huge smile. 'What are you doing here, darling? I was just about to pack up so I could meet you at home. How was the court case? I didn't hear from you and started to worry.'

'Oh, it was fine, but I'm going back to Wellington to get away for a while,' I burst out.

'What do you mean?' Liam looked puzzled.

'I can't explain it now. I need to go and pack.'

'Please don't do anything stupid, Stella. Please go home and wait for me. I'll only be fifteen minutes. We can talk about it when I get home.'

'I have to go,' I said and began running out the door.

It was six by the time I got home. I had thirty minutes to pack. Running to the bedroom to fetch the old suitcase from under the bed, I started frantically clearing my drawers and stuffing my clothes into the case. It was 6.20 pm and I needed to be at the airport by 7 pm to be eligible for the standby flight. As I began dragging my suitcase towards the front door, I heard a car pull up outside. Knowing it was probably Liam, I raced to the bathroom to grab my toothbrush and stuffed it in my handbag as Liam walked in the front door.

Taking in the suitcase, he looked at me in bemusement and asked, 'Why, why?'

'I can't explain it now. I have to be at the airport in thirty minutes.'

He moved towards me. 'Please don't go. Please can we talk about this?' Tears were running down his cheeks.

'I have to go. I'll miss my plane.' After I'd been in Wellington I sensed that I needed to run away. We had never really had a relationship of trust. To be honest, I didn't really think about why I was leaving or how long I would be gone.

'Can I take you to the airport? Please let me come with you.'

'You can take me but we need to go now.'

That was the longest car trip of my life. Liam would not stop crying, repeating over and over, 'Why? Please don't go.

I'm nothing without you. If you leave me, you know I'll go back to drugs. I can't stay clean without you.'

Fighting back the tears, I kept focused on the road, trying not to be swayed by my emotions. I felt so sad because I didn't want to hurt Liam; he was a good man and I knew he loved me, but I didn't know how I felt about him any more. The words Mark had said on the phone kept ringing in my head: 'You deserve better. You need to do something with your life.'

We arrived at the airport with ten minutes to spare before they would call me if there was a seat available. Those ten minutes almost saw me change my mind. 'Please don't leave me,' Liam repeated over and over again.

I was almost at the point of giving in, I couldn't take seeing Liam in so much pain, when a voice over the public address system announced, 'Calling Miss Stella Gibney to counter two, Miss Stella Gibney to counter two.' That was the sign I needed. I reached over to give Liam one last hug. 'I'll call you. I'll only be a few weeks.' I didn't tell him I had accepted a job on the ski fields—how could I? I never saw him again.

•

The following Friday I was on a bus heading to Mt Ruapehu. I had never been there before and had no idea what was ahead of me. I remember gazing out of the window and thinking, *How did I end up here?* I tried hard not to think about Liam, whether he was okay, whether I'd done the right thing. I felt as though I was in a dream where strange things kept happening to me, over which I had no control.

When I arrived at the ski lodge, I was shown to a small room with nothing more in it than a bed and handbasin, but it was pretty and I felt a wave of exhilaration that I was about to start a new life.

I began working as the nanny for the managers' children. After only a few short weeks one of the housemaids fell pregnant, so I asked if we could swap roles. The managers agreed and I began working with the other girls as a housemaid. We always had fun and partied hard every weekend at the only pub on the mountain. I don't recall thinking much about Liam over those three months. I felt free of the responsibilities my relationship with him had placed on me, and it felt good to be single after having been in long-term relationships since the age of fifteen.

Us girls would go to the pub and flirt with the ski instructors, although mostly they were after the female instructors or the visitors, not working-class housemaids like us. I was especially keen on one of the instructors, and one night I made my play for him. It was a Friday evening and we had the next day off, so we decided to a make a night of it, starting with tequila shots in my room. There were three of us, sitting on the floor, one after the other, knocking back shots until we had finished the whole bottle, then we headed to the pub. What happened next was not something I'm proud of. In fact, I felt terrible shame the next morning.

We staggered to the pub, grabbed a table and ordered more drinks. Over the course of the next hour, we became less and less coherent as the effects of the tequila started to kick in. 'I'm off now,' one of the girls said. She got up to leave and promptly collapsed in the doorway. Fortunately, she had a male friend who helped her up and took her home. I don't recall much of what happened next. Some time over the course of the night I ended up chatting with the guy I was keen on, and he asked me if I would like a ride back to the dorm. The last thing I remember was getting into a four-wheel drive with him and his friend and the two of them saying we were just going up the mountain for a drive first.

The next morning I woke up in his room with my clothes strewn all over the floor. I was alone and I could remember nothing beyond getting into the vehicle. We had drunk a whole bottle of tequila between three of us and I had just passed out. I had no recollection of events and I didn't really want to consider what had happened. Fortunately I didn't see that instructor again as the ski season ended just a few short weeks later.

Chapter Ten

I was twenty-one and my life seemed to be going nowhere. Then I managed to score a job as a sales representative for Wellington Newspapers, working in the auto classified section. I enjoyed the job and found it was something I was good at. My role involved going around to the car yards and taking photos for the paper, so I was out on the road every day, which I loved. It wasn't long before I met a new man, Peter. He was a radio announcer and he'd been out with my sister Rebecca for a short while. I felt humbled he would be interested in a plain girl like me. We had only been dating for three months when we moved in together. I was happy, although that wasn't to last long.

I was at the local pub with my sister Diana and a few work colleagues when I was approached by a woman I knew only vaguely. 'Hey Stella, how are you?' she said. 'Look, I really didn't want to say anything, but your boyfriend is sleeping with a friend of mine and I thought you should know.'

I was in shock. I ran to the bathroom, trying to hold back the tears. I shut myself in a cubicle and started sobbing. I heard the bathroom door open. 'Stella, are you in here?' It was Diana. 'Come on, you're going to move out tonight and I'm going to help you.'

She drove me to the flat, helped pack up my things and took me back to her place. *Why do men use me like this? I kept asking myself. Why can't I find someone to love me?* My relationship with Peter had only lasted four months, but the scars of having someone cheat on me lasted for years.

•

Before too long I met James, a radio journalist who was passionate about his job and loved the theatre. He was an amateur performer and would often appear in local plays. I liked him, and I was doing okay, and then, quite suddenly, my dad died.

Dad hadn't been well for many years, having had a second stroke. I didn't really know my father. I couldn't remember ever having had a real conversation with him. Mostly what I remembered about him was that he was someone to be feared because of his violent rages when we were growing up.

For years I was very afraid of Dad but as an adult I wish I had been able to get to know him, to discuss what mattered to him and what had occurred in his life that had made him the way he was. It makes me sad to think that I no longer have that opportunity. He was my dad and I loved him.

About twelve months earlier Dad had found a red patch on his foot. The doctors had told him he had an infection that was poisoning his bloodstream. A week later they'd amputated his leg just below the knee. The operation had been successful, although the doctors had said it was touch and go for a while as he almost died on the operating table. After months of rehabilitation, Dad had learned to walk again with the help of a prosthetic leg. He wasn't a fit man and had carried a bit of excess weight and being a heavy smoker and drinker all his life didn't help.

Rebecca had gone home to help Dad recover from his surgery. They developed a very close bond over the last few months of his life because he had to learn how to use a prosthetic leg. Rebecca was a huge support to Dad. Only a few months afterwards, however, Dad had noticed clotting starting to appear in his other foot. Mum had called the doctor to the house and Dad had been given the devastating news that they would have to remove his other leg.

It was around seven in the evening, the week Dad had been given the news, and for some reason I had the unexpected urge to visit my parents. James and I were on our way to the city to see a show, but I asked him if we could drop up to see Mum and Dad for a bit.

Mum was surprised to see us. 'What are you doing here on a Friday night?' she asked. 'Shouldn't you be partying in the city?'

'I just wanted to call over to see how Dad was and how he's taking the news the doctor gave him. Is he okay?'

'He's in bed. He said he had a bit of heartburn so I gave him a Panadol to make him feel better, but he's still awake. Go on up and see him.'

When I walked into the bedroom I found Dad sitting on the edge of his bed, staring down at the floor. 'Are you okay, Dad?' I asked.

'I don't think I'm going to make it through this operation,' he said with the saddest look in his eyes.

I put my arm around him and kissed him gently on the cheek. 'You're going to be okay, Dad.'

He looked at me with the sweetest smile on his old face and said the words I'd longed to hear all my life: 'I love you, Stella.'

Those were the last words he said to me.

James and I headed back into the city, going to the show, then on to a party. We didn't get home until 3 am. It had been a big night and I woke out of a deep sleep when someone began banging loudly on the window. 'Stella, Stella, are you in there?' It was my brother Patrick. Why on earth was he banging on my window at 6.30 in the morning? Hungover and still half asleep, I dragged myself out of bed to open the front door. Patrick and his wife Annie were standing on the step, looking so sad.

'Where have you been?' Patrick asked. 'We've been trying to call you all night.'

'What's wrong?' I asked, my heart leaping into my throat.

'It's Dad. I am so sorry, sis, but Dad had a massive heart attack last night and died.'

'No, that can't be true. I only saw him last night!'

Patrick moved towards me, stretching out his arms. He hugged me tight and I began to sob in his arms. *Why now?* I kept asking myself. Dad had told me he loved me for the first time last night. He had softened over the years, with the strokes and loss of his leg. Yes, he had been a tyrant, but I still loved him, and I'd thought that now I would have the chance to get to know him, but it was too late.

•

James was a great support through it all. Then he was promoted to a job in Auckland and although we had only been together a short time, he asked if I would go with him. It was no surprise I said yes—the word no had never been in my vocabulary—and so there I was on a train a few weeks later about to start a new life in yet another new city. I loved my job at Wellington Newspapers and they didn't want to lose me, so they created a new role for me in Auckland, working to establish a new feature in the classified section of the Sunday newspaper.

We had only been in Auckland a few months when I got the news that Patrick had been diagnosed with a brain tumour and was to be operated on in a few days. Patrick had been having migraines and spells of dizziness and had gone to the doctor for a check-up. After several blood tests and scans they'd found a tumour the size of a golf ball.

Back I went to Wellington. I will never forget the day of the operation. The whole family gathered at Patrick's bedside, assuring him that he was going to be okay. Annie, Patrick's wife, was pregnant with their first child but she was being positive too. They held hands tightly before the nurse came in to say it was time. We each leaned over our brother, kissing him goodbye, not knowing if this was the last time we would see him alive. They had shaved his head and he was in an operating gown, and my big brother looked small and vulnerable as they wheeled him off to theatre.

The next twelve hours were the longest to endure. Was the operation going to plan? Had they been able to remove the tumour successfully? And what of the risks? The doctors had said Patrick would almost certainly lose at least one of his senses even if the operation was successful, as the tumour was lodged in the centre where his hearing, taste, smell, touch and facial nerves were attached. It was a long wait, but after a gruelling twelve-hour operation Patrick was wheeled into recovery. The operation had been a success and miraculously Patrick had only suffered minor nerve damage.

•

Being back made me realise how much I missed living there, so I told James I was leaving and moving back to Wellington. As usual, I was in and out of relationships, all short-term. I was looking for someone, or something, to take away the emptiness I felt inside.

I applied for a job as sales representative for Rothmans Tobacco Company and, to my surprise, was successful. My role was to win showcases in shop fronts and plaster the entire frontage with Rothmans cigarette advertising. The job came with a brand-new company car and eight cartons of free cigarettes per month, which we were supposed to hand out in pubs and clubs in order to convert smokers to our brand.

Friday night was the highlight of my week, heading down to the local hotel where, of course, I would be on the lookout for Mr Right. After several weeks of listening to a new band, I thought I'd found him. Greg was the lead singer. He was a bit rough and rugged, which I was always attracted to, and he had the sweetest voice that had me mesmerised. I would sit listening to the band, dreaming of how beautiful it would be to have Greg sing love songs to me.

After the band had finished playing one night, they joined us at the table for a drink, as they often did. It was nearly closing time and I smiled over at Greg, hoping to capture his attention. Finally I asked if he would mind driving me home. He said yes, and I was thrilled. When he pulled up outside my house I leaned over and whispered, 'Would you like to come up?' Inside, I lured him into the bedroom—surely he would want me after he had been with me. We started making out on the bed. His touch was so warm and his kisses so sweet. I was in heaven. I gave all I could that night, hoping he would feel the love I felt. I was so used to doing that.

I wanted it to last but it was all over way too quickly. Greg turned over onto his side and mumbled something. 'What did you say?' I asked, and leaned over to wrap my arms around him, hoping he would reach out and hold me in return.

'This is wrong, I shouldn't be here,' he said.

'What is wrong?' I didn't understand what he meant.

'I shouldn't be here,' he said again, and stood up, pulling on his pants.

'What do you mean? What did I do wrong?'

'Nothing,' he replied. 'I'm in love with someone and I didn't want this.' Then he walked out of the door and out of my life.

I cried myself to sleep, and the next morning the spiral began. I couldn't live with the feelings of worthlessness anymore. What was wrong with me? Where had I gone wrong? I would play Greg's album over and over again, torturing myself, knowing he was singing love songs to someone else. I began to slide into a state of deep depression. I wanted to end my life. I thought death would stop the pain. I thought I was worthless, born to fail. I told myself I was not attractive enough and no one was ever going to love me.

I couldn't go to work. I locked myself in my room, crying all day and night. I couldn't eat, and my weight plummeted. I wouldn't talk to anyone. I felt as though my whole world had fallen apart and there was no one who could rescue me. One day I took twelve painkillers all at once in an attempt to ease my pain, but all that did was make me sleep. Mum was at a loss as to what to do, and the entire family was worried about me. This was the lowest point of my life. I was unlovable and I wanted to end it all. I could no longer bear the pain.

One night Mum knocked on my door with a Bible in her hand. 'It might help if you read this,' she said in her gentle voice.

How could that help? I thought. *No one loves me. I am unlovable. Even God can't love me.*

I flung open the Bible and the first words I saw were: 'I have loved you with an everlasting love.' I could not believe what I was reading. Those were the words I had been longing to hear all my life. Immediately I felt a strange sense of peace.

The next day it was Patrick's birthday. Mum had asked him over for dinner. He was a born-again Christian and had always seemed a bit too intense with it for my liking. Years ago, when we'd shared a flat, he'd talk to me about Jesus but I'd wanted nothing to do with it.

It was early evening and I could hear the family gathering downstairs. Then there was a knock on the door. 'Can I come in?' It was Patrick. He had been concerned about me these past weeks and he wanted to see how I was. Patrick was, and still is, an amazing brother and he had been through a lot in his own life. News of his brain tumour hadn't encouraged him to give up on his faith; instead he had been inspired to live his life to the full.

He walked into my bedroom and turned on the light. 'Why don't you come downstairs and join us?' he asked gently.

'I can't, I can't,' I replied, and began crying all over again.

'Oh Stella, don't you know that God loves you? If you want your life to turn around, you just need to ask Jesus into your life. Can I pray for you?' he asked.

What did I have to lose? I was at the lowest point in my life. I remembered the words I had read the day before. I nodded and moved forward to the end of the bed.

Patrick placed his hand on my head and began to pray. As he did so, I felt as though someone was pouring warm water all over me. When I opened my eyes, it was almost as if the room had grown lighter, as if I was somewhere else. I somehow felt alive in a way I never had before, and afterwards I was able to follow Patrick downstairs to share in the celebrations.

My life changed dramatically that night. I felt at peace in my heart. Although there was still pain from my past I was yet to deal with, I felt a security I had never known. I understood that my life was going to be okay now.

Chapter Eleven

I was passionate about my new-found faith in God, and was determined to make a new life for myself, so I started attending the church Patrick had been going to for years. It was a small Baptist church that had undergone some amazing changes in recent years. The most significant of these was what was known back then as the Life in the Spirit movement. As a child we had attended church and I remembered the services as being very proper and boring. Now, thanks to this new movement, services were enlivened by a five-piece band and we would sing modern praise songs, often clapping and dancing to the beat.

Sundays became my favourite day of the week. I had church in the morning, followed by lunch at Bethel House.

Bethel House was run by Ray and Margaret Belesky, the parents of Patrick's wife, Annie. They were elders at the church and had a ministry of caring for the disadvantaged and underprivileged. It was a place of refuge for everyone. Bethel House sat on a massive block of land surrounded by tall trees, and it had a long, sweeping driveway. The house was huge, with an enormous wooden staircase in the foyer circling to the upstairs rooms. The kitchen and dining rooms were always buzzing with people. We would spend our Sunday afternoons sitting around sharing our lives, often laughing over jokes or playing board games or charades. At last I felt as though I belonged.

At the time I was still working for Rothmans. I enjoyed the work but found I no longer wanted to smoke, or to encourage other people to smoke. The job was getting in the way of how I wanted to live my life, so it was easy to make the decision to quit.

In December 1983 a group of us from church went on a weekend camping trip to Hawkes Bay. I was introduced to Kieran, a handsome, athletic man, with tanned skin and a cheeky smile. My initial reaction was, *Oh, I'm not sure about you*—perhaps I was finally learning some caution where handsome men were concerned!

We were on our way to a white-water rafting trip on the Tuki Tuki River. We had been warned to be careful and to listen closely to the instructors. The week before there had been a drowning on the same stretch of water. Although we had been given the all-clear by the rafting company, the waters were still extremely treacherous.

At first, riding the rapids felt like riding ocean waves on a body board, but as we moved further downstream the white water became increasingly turbulent.

The instructor yelled, 'Paddle to the left, paddle to the left!' as we headed towards a waterfall. 'Faster! Harder! We need to go to the left of that rock ahead!'

We paddled as fast as we could, trying desperately to keep the raft from moving to the right, but the water was too powerful. It all happened in a matter of seconds. We hit the rock and ploughed over the waterfall. The raft was flipped upside down and we were plunged into the maelstrom at the base of the waterfall. My life flashed before me as I tumbled upside down underneath the boat as if I was in a washing machine. The water was too powerful. It was hopeless trying to find air as my body was flung about. I was panicking. I realised I was drowning. I began to sink, then suddenly I felt a strong arm wrap around my waist, clenching me tight. My rescuer, the instructor, forced me to the surface and grabbed a rope from the side of the upturned raft, holding tightly to me at the same time.

The group from the raft in front of us were on the embankment watching all this unfold, and they hurled ropes to the raft and winched it to the shoreline. Everyone was safe but very shaken. None of us wanted to get back in the raft, but we had to—the cliff face was too steep and there was no way back on foot. Scared and trembling, we set off again into the next set of rapids.

I was in shock. I sat holding fast to the side of the raft, praying that God would keep us safe. As we approached the next set of rapids we started paddling furiously, trying to steer the raft in the right direction. The current was impossibly strong, and we headed straight towards the cliff face, jamming the raft up against rocks. We all managed to jump out onto the small ledge of the cliff, still holding tight to the ropes of the raft. We had to tip the raft up to empty it of water. Frightened and even more shaken, we pulled together and finally it was empty. We then had to scramble back into place and tackle the remaining rapids.

We made it through the last set of rapids unscathed, pulling up to the riverbank where the rest of the rafters were waiting. It's hard to describe how I was feeling: a mixture of relief but fear at the same time. Every time I closed my eyes I could feel myself out of control, as if I was in that washing machine again, spinning round and around. I couldn't shake it off.

We were all a little fragile on the trip home. The excitement and exhilaration we had felt on the way up to the river had been replaced by a mood of solemn reflection. We each shared our experiences of the ride, the terror and the utter helplessness of being tossed about at the mercy of the river. Kieran had been in our raft, and as I listened to him speak of his experience I thought, *Oh, perhaps I was wrong about you*. Little did I know.

•

Kieran started attending church more regularly after our rafting experience and eventually he plucked up the courage to ask me out. We were inseparable those first few weeks. I was living in a shared flat at the back of the church and Kieran was still living at home, so we would go for long drives just to get some time alone. Looking back, this wasn't the smartest thing to do because, in trying to right the wrongs of my past, I wanted to 'save myself' until we were married. Alone together at night in a parked car was way too tempting for us both. I guess that's why it was only three months later that Kieran proposed. Of course I said yes. We had known each other for eight months. Kieran was twenty-two years old and I was twenty-four.

We were married at Miramar Christian Centre on Saturday 25 August 1984, in front of around forty people, and afterwards had a small afternoon tea at the church. We had a candle ceremony after taking our vows: we both held a single small candle, which we were to blow out before we lit a larger candle; this was to signify the two of us becoming one. Interestingly, Kieran didn't blow out his candle. Perhaps I should have read this as a sign.

I was having counselling at Bethel. It was helping me to see that I had some deep-seated feelings that needed to be dealt with. Some of these feelings related to my relationship with my younger sister, Rebecca.

I don't know if you have ever felt jealousy, but I sure did, and I felt it towards Rebecca. I was four years old when Rebecca was born. I went from being the youngest of five and the focus of everyone's attention, to being a big sister who had to give up her cherished place in the family to a new baby. I didn't know it was jealousy then, I just knew that when Rebecca came into the world I somehow didn't feel special any more.

By the time I went to school, Mum was able to work part-time and had a little extra cash. It seemed that this money was spent mainly on Rebecca. I was particularly jealous of her dance classes. When I was little there'd been hardly enough money for food, let alone after-school activities. I know if she'd been able to, Mum would have given us all the same opportunities, but this didn't make the unfairness easier to deal with.

When Rebecca turned sixteen, I took her under my wing, as big sisters do, and went out nightclubbing with her. As we put on our makeup in the bathroom I would look in the mirror at myself, then at Rebecca, who had a beautiful heart-shaped face, gorgeous blue eyes and long thick wavy hair, and I'd feel that I just couldn't measure up. By the time we would get to the nightclub, I'd be convinced I didn't look very good, and sure enough I would sit at the table waiting for someone to ask me to dance, while Rebecca would have them lining up for her. We attended a modelling course together and the results spoke for themselves. Rebecca finished with an A+ while I finished with a B-. It confirmed to me I just didn't have what she had. I resented her for that, but I didn't know it was resentment. She seemed to have everything I didn't have, and I thought that was my lot in life.

In a counselling session I was asked to think about the way I felt about myself, and Rebecca's name unexpectedly popped into my head. I went home and started to talk to God about my relationship with my sister, and all of a sudden I began to cry. Why was she more popular than I was? Why did she get everything she wanted? Why was she prettier than me? As I cried, I realised how deep the pain was and I understood that Rebecca was not to blame for it. After a few more tears and letting go, I knew I needed to see her.

It was midday and the small coffee shop we'd arranged to meet in was getting busy. I arrived before Rebecca and sat down by the window. As I looked at my watch, my heart started to beat faster. How would she react when I told her how I felt? Would she hate me for it?

Just then Rebecca walked in, shaking off the light rain from her coat and swinging it over the back of her chair. 'Sorry I am a bit late, dearie. Traffic was a bit heavy. Did you want to eat or just have coffee?'

We ordered and small-talked until our coffee arrived—I didn't want what I had to say to be interrupted. 'There's something I need to say to you, sis,' I said, my eyes beginning to fill with tears. 'I'm so sorry but I've resented you for years. I have felt like you have everything—you were more popular at school, more intelligent and much prettier than me—and because I have felt that way, I've held resentment towards you. I know it's not your fault. I'm just so sorry it has caused us not to be as close as I want to be. Can you forgive me?' As I looked up from wiping my tears with the napkin, I could see tears rolling down Rebecca's face.

'Oh Stella, I'm so sorry. I had no idea you've felt that way, because all my life I've wanted to be like you. You're always so kind and gentle, and I've always looked up to you.'

I was shocked. Here was my sister, who was gorgeous, talented and in demand as a model, and she had feelings of insecurity too.

I am so glad I made the decision to be vulnerable that day. It changed our relationship. We had always been close, but now that closeness had a depth to it, and it has only strengthened over the years. I thanked God for helping me to face my resentment. My beautiful mum, from as early as I can remember, taught us to forgive and let go. It sounds simple, but we waste years of our lives being emotionally crippled, held back by resentment towards people and events, until we learn to forgive.

Chapter Twelve

Kieran and I were living in a small flat in Hataitai and I had resumed working for Wellington Newspapers, while Kieran was working at the post office. One of the things we had in common was our desire to reach out to young people. After talking at length to the church pastors, we were given the go-ahead to open a teenage drop-in centre on Friday nights. We applied for government funding, gained approval and opened 'the Den' a few weeks later. It was a place where teenagers could play pool, table tennis, listen to music, or just hang out. We were in our element. I identified with these kids. Now I had a better life and I wanted to share my experiences with them and help them.

We had only been married a year when we decided to try for a baby. Kieran's dad hadn't been well for some time and we wanted his grandchild to be born while he was still alive. It wasn't long before I fell pregnant, but unfortunately, by the time I was to give birth, Kieran's dad had passed away, so he never got to meet our firstborn, Joshua.

I was two weeks overdue when I had my first contraction. By the time they were six minutes apart, I was admitted to hospital. For some reason, though, our baby didn't want to come out. I was sent on long walks, had warm baths and was given back massages by Kieran to try to relieve the pain. After a long twenty-four hours, I was fully dilated and was about to begin the final stages of giving birth, when all of a sudden Kieran pulled away from me, looking as white as a ghost. 'I'm so sorry, I'm going to be sick,' he announced, and dashed towards the bathroom. A minute or so later, and after yet another painful contraction, Kieran reappeared. 'I'm so sorry, I couldn't stand seeing you in so much pain,' he said sheepishly.

Just then the nurse said, 'All right, Stella, it's time to push again. I can see the head.'

Are there any words to describe the pain of that one last push, when you feel like you are being split in two? Thankfully, that push saw our beautiful baby boy come into the world. Josh finally made his entrance at 2.20 am on 29 May 1986. The nurse wrapped him in a blanket and passed him to me. It was like nothing else I had ever experienced. I felt that this was what I was here for, to be a mum and to have a child. It was utter joy. Kieran was beaming. It was only after counselling later down the track that I was able to allow myself to think about Chris and all I had to give up.

By 3.30 am I was back in the ward and in bed. Josh was safe in the crib next to me and I closed my eyes to sleep. It wasn't long before I was awoken by a nurse tapping me on the shoulder. 'I'm sorry to wake you, but we need to take Josh for a while. He's okay, just go back to sleep and we will bring him to you in the morning.'

I tried to sleep but was aware of the empty crib. Kieran was asleep next to me in the huge recliner armchair that was available for anyone wanting to stay the night. I woke him up to tell him what had happened, but he reassured me that Josh would be fine and I should try to get some sleep.

At 6.30 am I was really starting to worry, when a nurse appeared with a clipboard. When I asked her where Josh was and when I could see him, she said, 'You can see him soon. The doctor just needs to explain a few things to you first.' I sat there frozen for the next few minutes, anxiously waiting for the doctor. What on earth was wrong? Josh had seemed fine when the nurse had taken him a few hours ago.

Finally the doctor walked in. He appeared calm as he stood at the foot of the bed. 'Hello, I'm Doctor Fraser and I'm here to talk to you about your son Josh. I have made a few notes and will explain everything to you in detail. When the nurse came in to check on Josh at 4 am, he appeared to be grey in colour, so she took him to the paediatric ward for observation. That was when I was called. His condition is fragile at the moment and I need to explain to you what will happen next. I have drawn a diagram of what we think is happening to baby Josh.'

I could barely take in what he was saying.

'We have detected a problem with Josh's heart. It is what we call TGA—transposition of the great artery.'

He went on to explain in more detail but all I heard was that Josh would need open-heart surgery because this was a potentially fatal heart condition.

I sat there in shock, not knowing what to think. Why Josh? Why had God allowed this to happen to us?

When the doctor had finished explaining, he said we could go and visit Josh. I felt my knees buckle as I pulled myself up off the bed; I was shaking, not knowing what to expect. It was relatively quiet on the ward as we approached the nurses' station.

'Hello, we're Josh's mum and dad,' said Kieran. 'Can we see him?'

'Of course. He has slept a bit, but we have to wake him every few hours to test his blood. He is in the room around the corner, follow me,' she said in a gentle voice.

We followed her around the corner, but there was only one room, with a solid door, above which read *Intensive Care*.

My heart began to pound. Inside Intensive Care there were three incubators, each holding a tiny baby.

'Josh is over here,' the nurse whispered.

We understood the seriousness of our baby's condition when we saw his tiny body attached to all sorts of plugs and wires and monitors. He had a huge bandage wrapped around his tiny arm to hold the drip in place. He had cotton muslin pads covering his eyes. The nurse opened the glass porthole door of the incubator. 'You can touch him,' she said.

My hand was shaking and my eyes filled with tears as I reached in to touch my precious baby boy.

We sat there for the next two hours, taking turns just to touch him.

Eventually the doctor returned. 'I'm sorry, but we have to move fast now. We need to get Josh to Auckland Hospital,' which was the only hospital in New Zealand that had a heart monitor that could detect Josh's condition. 'We will have an ambulance transport you to the Wellington airport at 3.30 pm, where the air ambulance will fly the three of you to Auckland. It might be an idea to go back to the ward to pack your things, as you may be gone for a few days.'

Back at the ward, we found Mum, Patrick and Annie waiting for us. In tears, I began to recall the last few hours for them, explaining that Josh was to undergo open-heart surgery.

'We will get the church praying, Stella. Just hold on to God and He will carry you through this,' Patrick said, and bowed his head in prayer. 'Father God, thank you for wee

Josh, thank you that you have your hand on his life and have a plan for him. Uphold Stella and Kieran as they look to you, trusting that Josh is in your care. We pray for a miracle, that you will heal Josh. Amen.'

I felt a slight sense of relief as I began to hold on to the words Patrick had spoken.

After they had left, Kieran went home to pack some belongings, leaving me alone in the hospital room. 'Dear God,' I begged, 'please speak to me, give me words of comfort, help me to trust you.'

I reached over for my Bible. I opened it at Psalms: 'I look to the heavens where my help will come.' A sense of calm washed over me. God was in control and I needed to trust Him.

That afternoon the ambulance was waiting for us in the emergency bay, the nurse and doctor already on board. The nurse was perched next to Josh, who had been transferred to a smaller incubator. At the airport we were taken to a Piper Cherokee. Josh was placed carefully on a fold-down seat. I was told to sit at the back and Kieran was up the front next to the pilot.

Just after takeoff, the alarm on the small incubator went off, sending my heart into a panic. 'What is it? Is he okay?' I cried.

'Oh, yes, he's fine,' said the nurse. 'It's just the silly monitor going off. It does that sometimes on these flights. It's nothing to worry about.'

We arrived at Auckland airport about an hour and a half later and were met by an ambulance that took us to the paediatric cardiac ward at Auckland Hospital. Because it was an intensive care ward for children, rooms were available for mothers, so I secured a bed in a small room, sharing with another mother. The hospital had accommodation for fathers a five-minute walk away, so Kieran could stay close.

I didn't sleep well that night, although I was absolutely exhausted. Every time I heard a baby cry, I thought it was Josh, so I would get out of bed and make my way down the corridor to check whether he was okay.

The following morning, they checked his condition on the heart monitor and were puzzled by the fact they could find no evidence of the TGA. It was a huge relief for both Kieran and I, although Josh's condition was still quite serious as his blood levels were way out of whack and a transfusion might be necessary. His tiny heels were like pincushions, as they had to prick them every three hours to check his blood. He would scream as they tried to extract another drop of blood. As a mum, it was heartbreaking to watch. I felt absolutely helpless.

In that long and emotional week, I learned that life is precious and to cherish every minute I have with my children. We never know what tomorrow may bring. By day six, Josh's blood levels had stabilised and he was cleared of any heart condition. We were free to fly home. It was a miracle and I still thank God every day for saving my beautiful boy's life.

Two years later, I fell pregnant with our second son. Jeremy, whom we've called Jem since he was a toddler, was born on 5 May 1988. He was a healthy, happy baby and never any trouble. Our little family was complete. Kieran began an electrical apprenticeship; we had two amazing little boys; we attended a wonderful church and had some great friends. Life was good.

Chapter Thirteen

In January 1989 Kieran and I decided to make the big move to Australia, where we were to settle in Melbourne. Our goal was to be missionaries, and with Kieran's trade we could go pretty much anywhere in the world. We thought Australia would be a good stepping stone.

We started attending Blackburn Baptist Church, where we were welcomed by the pastor and his wife. We instantly felt at home there and we made friends easily. Kieran got a job with a local electrician, so he could finish the last two years of his apprenticeship, and we rented a lovely house with a huge backyard for the children.

During our time in Melbourne, my mum came to stay. She would come to church with us, often joining us if we were invited somewhere afterwards for lunch. One Sunday Kieran was adamant he didn't want Mum to come. When I told Mum, she was hurt, but I felt I couldn't do anything about that. This seemed to shift something in me, though, because over the next little while she was with us, we no longer saw eye to eye on a lot of small things and a distance sprang up between us.

I knew in my heart I had to deal with this, whatever it was. I grabbed a notepad and pen and started to write down how I was feeling. I knew I had to get it out, to understand what I was feeling and why. That was the first time I realised there was healing in writing. I had started to write all those years ago in the Sounds but had done nothing since then. All my feelings came pouring out. *Dear God, I have so many mixed emotions that I don't know where to start. Mum and I aren't getting on and I'm really sad and mad at the same time . . . I love her but she has hurt me.*

This hurt from the past was deep and I really felt the need to express it and get it down on paper. Once I started I couldn't stop, I had to keep writing. It was as though there was someone listening to me as I poured out my heart. I found myself reliving painful childhood memories of times when I felt Mum had let me down. There was no escaping it, there it was in black and white, staring back at me. Five painful events that had taken place as a child, one from as young as five years old, that I had buried, memories my mum would have no idea about. As I wrote about each one, the pain that had been buried deep began to surface. I cried as I uncovered the hidden things in my heart. Mum had kept making excuses for Dad and I just wanted her to make excuses for me.

It was painful, but also one of the most freeing things I have ever experienced. When I finally put the pen down, I felt such relief, even though my eyes were sore from crying and my heart heavy with all the pain. I was free, but now I needed to forgive Mum. Don't get me wrong here, my mum has been a fantastic mum, still is to this day, and I know she didn't mean to hurt me. Being a mum myself, I can recall times when I have said or done things that would have hurt my boys, and that causes me pain, but we are human and we all make mistakes. We just need to ask those we hurt to forgive us. Hopefully they can and they will.

At last the pain was now gone and I felt free. I spoke with Mum and our relationship went to a much deeper level. Maybe, unknowingly, I had held her at arm's length all those years, because of the pain I had buried inside.

Not only was it great that Mum and I were friends again, I had discovered something amazing. I could write all my emotions down and find understanding, release and freedom. I had probably spent three days on and off writing about Mum, but it had simply poured out of me. I knew there was a hurting little girl inside me who needed a voice. My writing could give that little girl the chance to be heard.

I could say what I wanted on paper and nobody would judge me.

•

The months passed, and we were busy with home group, friends and church. Going to church always made me feel as though I wasn't alone, that I was cared for, both by God and by the church community. We would often have friends over for dinner or be invited out. The boys seemed happy too. I loved that Rebecca lived in Melbourne now. We would catch up when she wasn't busy with her television and film work, chatting on the phone, or she would pop over for a visit. Rebecca was working on *Flying Doctors*, *Come In Spinner* and *All Together Now*, which were hugely successful. She was becoming a household name. She was always my close friend and dear sister. I'm enormously proud of her for the person she is.

Kieran was progressing well at work. He didn't earn much as a second-year apprentice, but it was enough to cover rent and food. We knew it wasn't long before he would be fully qualified, then he would be on good money. Like most couples, we'd had our share of disagreements in the first few years of our marriage, but our arguments began to intensify while we were living in Melbourne. The arguments always seemed to be about the same thing: Kieran thought I was trying to control him and I thought he didn't love me. I felt that each time we argued we lost something we couldn't get back. We went for counselling, but it didn't seem to help. I turned to my journal, a safe place where I could speak honestly without fear of being rejected.

> *Well, today is Friday and I am sitting in our modern home in Melbourne feeling low. The children are outside playing, with seemingly not a care in the world. How I wish I was a child right now and didn't have to deal with the pain of being an adult. Kieran has been out for a few hours now after we had another argument this morning. It all seems so pointless, the pain we cause each other. It's the same old argument: I am mothering him and making all the decisions. I have lost count of the amount of times we have had this argument. I see the anger inside him towards me and it hurts. I can't get close to him. It's as if he has built a huge brick wall around himself.*

Although journalling didn't change what was going on around me, it did highlight areas of my life that I needed to change, and if I was being completely honest with myself, then I would often see the ugly side of my behaviour that I needed to address. Then on other days, my journalling would reflect happier experience, like the time my sister arrived with a tape she had made for me.

Rebecca brought me an unexpected present. It was a tape she'd made for me, of a song she said made her think of me. It was Bette Midler's 'Wind Beneath My Wings'.

Listening to the words, that song still makes me cry with gratitude that I have such a special relationship with my beautiful sister. The song perfectly expresses that Rebecca was in the spotlight and I was in the shadows.

•

A few weeks had passed when I picked up my journal and began to write, *Kieran and I have been arguing again and it hurts when he calls me names. Why doesn't he love me? Why is it so hard for anyone to love me? Everyone in my life seems to have hurt me. Why am I so unlovable?* After writing another four tear-stained pages I stopped and closed my eyes. 'Why, God, why do I feel so sad inside?' What happened next took me by complete surprise. A vivid visual image came into my mind. It was a picture of a heart with several arrows in it, the kind you see in old cowboy movies. Blood was flowing freely from the arrow wounds and dripping onto the ground. Each arrow had fletching at the end, with something printed on it, but I couldn't see what it was.

As I looked again I saw an arrow on the ground; all that remained of where it had been lodged in the heart was a small scar. The word on the fletching was *MUM*. 'What does this mean?' I asked. A still, small voice answered me. 'This is a visual image of your heart, and the arrows represent all the people in your life who have hurt you deeply. The frill on the end holds the names of each of those people, and the reason you can't see the names yet is that you will go on a journey of healing and eventually, when the time for healing has come, you will find out the names of each person.'

'But what is that arrow on the ground, and why is Mum's name printed on it?'

'That arrow represents the pain you went through as a child with your mum, but since you have forgiven your mum the heart wound has healed and the arrow has no power to hurt you any longer.'

I began to understand the enormous power of journalling that day. Not only did I realise that I carried hidden pain from my past, but also that I was living like a wounded soldier. I knew I needed heart surgery to repair the damage that had been done in my life.

I needed to forgive those who had hurt me, like the man who had sexually assaulted me when I was six years old. I was still blaming God for allowing that to happen to me. Ultimately I thought God didn't love me as much as He loved other people. I was never quite good enough growing up. I wasn't good at school and certainly didn't feel very attractive, and I had believed from an early age that I was on this planet to be used by men. My earliest memory was of watching my father drag my mother around the house by her hair, screaming and yelling abuse at her.

We used to go and visit my Mum's parents, Nana and Granddad, in Wellington. I never felt right when we went there. I knew there was something about Granddad that wasn't safe. My sister Diana and I would share a bed. 'I'll stay awake while you sleep,' she would say. 'Then I'll wake you up so I can sleep.' The toilet door had a half window and we would see his shape outside the door when we were having a bath or when we went to the toilet. We used to put toilet paper in the keyhole so he couldn't see us on the toilet. At the time we thought it was just the way Granddad was. It wasn't until we were older that my sisters Teresa and Diana, who had other experiences with my grandfather, realised how wrong it was. We never spoke to Mum about any of this until then. She was devastated.

Years later when my grandfather lay dying, my mother was at his bedside. She had endured many years of sexual abuse from him as a child, something that I only learned about as an adult. As he took his final breaths she leaned into him and whispered, 'I forgive you.' He responded with the words that would break my mother's heart. 'For what?' he said. He refused to acknowledge that he had ever done anything wrong. He died shortly after.

Chapter Fourteen

It was a cool Melbourne winter's morning. I was making Jem's bed when a thought popped into my head. *How lovely it would be to own our own home.* Where had that come from? I had never entertained the idea. I knew it was not possible to save for a deposit on Kieran's wage, yet the thought stayed with me all day. I was daydreaming about it as I went about my chores. I couldn't wait for Kieran to get home to talk to him about it. When I brought it up, Kieran dismissed the idea as impossible. However, that didn't stop us talking about where we could afford to buy, if ever the opportunity came up. We looked at house prices in Melbourne, but they were way out of our reach. Brisbane seemed to offer an affordable alternative. It was a bonus that my brother Patrick and sister Teresa, whom I hadn't seen since she'd left New Zealand when I was fifteen, both lived in Brisbane.

My excitement faded over the next few days as I looked realistically at our financial situation. I had almost given up on the idea when I had a call from Rebecca. 'Are you home this afternoon?' she asked.

'Yeah, why aren't you working?'

'Oh, I'm on my way, but there's something I have for you and I want to drop it off.'

I hung up the phone and wondered what it was she wanted to give me. I was convinced by the time she knocked on the door that she had gone through her wardrobe and had a few choice hand-me-downs for me. I always loved having her old clothes; she was so well dressed and everything she bought was good quality, so I was looking forward to seeing what she had for me this time.

I opened the door to find Rebecca standing there with just a small bag over her shoulder. No hand-me-downs in there.

'Hi, dearie, come in.'

'I can't stay. I just needed to give you something.'

'What's this?' I asked awkwardly as she passed me an envelope.

'Well, I was paying a few bills when I suddenly thought I heard a voice saying, "You need to write a cheque for

Stella and Kieran for five thousand dollars." I laughed at the voice and said, "Now that's a bit much. How about half that?" But the voice came back, "No, I want you to write it for five thousand dollars." "Okay then, you win." So here it is!'

I opened the envelope to find the cheque inside and burst into tears. 'Oh dear, I can't take this much.'

'But you have to,' she said. 'I've already had that argument with the man upstairs and He insisted. Anyway, I have to fly, but I'll call you in a few days.' And off she went.

Closing the door behind me, I walked over to the table and sat down. I was in shock. I could not believe what I was holding in my hands: this was the deposit for a house.

•

Three months later, we were living in Brisbane. At first we thought we had made a terrible mistake because Kieran couldn't get a job and had to apply for the dole. Financially we were going backwards, then the Queensland Government introduced a joint housing scheme that enabled us to move into our own home. The initiative was introduced for low income earners who didn't have the full deposit or ability to repay a full mortgage, and with our remaining cash we were able to put down a small deposit. It was my dream house: a modern, high-set home at the end of a cul-de-sac with an outdoor spa and barbecue area. It was all I had ever hoped for—a comfortable home we could raise our family in.

We enrolled Josh in kindy at a small local Christian school and we started going to a local church, Gateway Baptist, where we made a few good friends. Everything seemed to be perfect, apart from the fact that Kieran and I were still arguing. He hadn't been able to find a job, so the only alternative was for me to go back to work. I really didn't want to, but we were starting to fall behind in our mortgage repayments. Within a few weeks I had secured a job as an area sales executive for a local newspaper, the *Reporter*. It was a tough sell as the retail market was slow and I had targets to achieve. I also hated not being at home for the boys. It broke my heart leaving them every morning. We asked my mum to come and live with us for a few months to help out while I worked, which was both a blessing and difficult at the same time.

Unfortunately, as hard as we tried, we couldn't get ourselves out of the financial slump. A few weeks later we drove to Melbourne and stayed with friends, hoping to talk through a few things to try and make sense of our situation. We went to church on the Sunday and after the service we were chatting with friends in the foyer when one of the youth pastors approached us and asked if we had considered applying for the role of house parents for the halfway house. 'You guys would be great at that.'

The role of house parents was to get the 'adopted' kids up in the morning, care for them, and nurture them just as parents would. We made an appointment to see the pastor and within a few days of returning to Brisbane we received a letter of acceptance for the role. We were both excited about the year ahead; we knew we would face plenty of challenges but we were sure it was the right thing to do.

It was actually a relief to sell our share of the house back to the government. The burden of debt was gone. We were back in Melbourne within a few weeks.

•

The halfway house where we were to live was old but full of character. On the pathway leading to the front door was a huge oak tree overhanging a covered verandah. On the verandah was an old green three-seater couch. That couch would often be a refuge from the noise and constant activity in the house over the following twelve months.

The house was large, with five bedrooms, an open-plan living room, a kitchen and a dining area with a huge table that could seat twelve. It was rare that the table wasn't crowded at dinner times. Kieran and I and the boys had separate accommodation at the front of the house, which allowed us to escape the hustle and bustle of the main house.

We settled in over the next few days before the girls arrived. Then, one by one, we met our 'adopted' children for the next six months: four girls, aged between sixteen and twenty-two. Sometimes I would be up until two or three in the morning just listening to the girls. It was enormously rewarding to be able to play a part in these teenagers' lives.

Those months were to be some of the most challenging of my life as I juggled being a mother to my two small boys, cooking every night and trying to build relationships with four teenage girls.

Kieran and I were arguing regularly again (behind closed doors, of course). The strain of it all was taking its toll. I believe we did have a positive impact on those girls, but at what cost to our marriage? After caring for the girls, the next six months were a breeze with four boys between sixteen and twenty-one. Girls can be hard work sometimes. I think I may be lucky I had sons!

Chapter Fifteen

At the end of the year, we needed to find a house to rent, as our time as house parents was ending. Michael and Moira, members of our church, had bought another house and were moving out of their home in Blackburn. It was a good family home and we settled in quickly. My relationship with Kieran was not getting any better, however. I knew we needed counselling and suggested we go together. Our pastor suggested a Christian counsellor named Sue and I made an appointment.

After our first session Kieran decided he didn't want to go but I continued to regularly see Sue and she worked on rebuilding my shattered self-esteem. On one visit Sue asked me how often I was intimate with Kieran.

'Oh, probably three or four times a week,' I said.

'What?' she replied. 'Even after you've been arguing?'

'Umm, yes. I've always given in to him when we get into bed, but it's nothing romantic after a fight, just doing the deed really.'

'How does that make you feel?' Sue asked with a slight frown on her face.

'Not very good, like I am being used, but that's pretty much my life story. I've never said no to a man when it comes to sex.' And there it was, the truth about what I felt I had to do to be loved. That was the beginning of my understanding my feelings about myself. It was as though I believed I had been put on this planet as a pleasure machine for men.

The task Sue gave me for the next few weeks was to identify why I felt like this. I knew where it had all begun, and I knew I had experienced some healing from the sexual abuse I suffered as a child, so why did I still act as though I was a slave to it? After many hours of journalling, combined with regular visits to the counsellor, I began to understand. Even though I had experienced healing for many of the actual events, I never really realised just how much impact all of these episodes had on me collectively until one entry in the middle of my counselling read as follows:

Monday 10 January
I've woken up this morning feeling really tired and sad at the same time. As I write this I wonder where I went

wrong in life, like my whole life has been a mistake. I have been having bad dreams too. Last night I was falling in the sea, going down, down, down to almost the bottom when I suddenly woke, feeling frightened. Eventually I went back to sleep only to wake with a fright after dreaming of two men pursuing me. They were running after me with knives trying to rape and murder me. Why am I dreaming like this, what does it mean? It seems like all my life I have felt powerless to overcome anything or anyone who attacks me. Like my earliest memories of the sexual abuse, the man who stole my innocence, then watching my dad beat my mum, and my grandfather, who we were scared of because he tried to touch us when no one was looking. At aged twelve, when I was sitting in the water at the beach and a guy (one of my girlfriend's brother's friends) came up behind me, sitting down, placing his legs either side of me, then began touching me under the water so no one could see. At age thirteen when I was raped on the beach, I kept saying no, then at age fourteen having to sneak into Brenton's room at night to have sex with him. Then one day I was walking along the street in broad daylight in Wellington city when a man in his twenties came running up behind me, throwing his hand up under my skirt, grabbing me between my legs and running off. Then the countless relationships I had with men who I allowed to abuse me sexually, men who would love me then leave me.

*Now I am in a marriage where I feel totally unloved
and rejected, but I continue to have sex with him. Why?
Maybe that is all I feel I am worth. I feel totally powerless
to overcome these feelings. I know in my head I am valued
because the Bible says so, and I know in my head God
loves me, so why do I not feel it?*

The very next day, I had another appointment with Sue.
'So, how are you feeling today?' she asked, ushering me
to a chair. 'You look a little weary, and as if you have
been crying.'

I could feel the tears welling up in my eyes again at Sue's
caring tone. 'It feels like my whole life I have been dedicated
to being who I think someone else wants me to be, and that
includes being available for men sexually. I've realised that
I've felt powerless to be anyone other than the person I've
become for everyone else.'

'Well now, that's a big step forward for you,' Sue said.
'Even though it's painful, it's important to identify your
thoughts about yourself. Because now you've identified them,
we can work out how to change them, so you begin to feel
valued and loved for the special person you are.'

A sense of relief washed over me. She understood, and
what's more, she had a plan to undo all the negativity in
my thinking and replace it with positive affirmation and a
deeper belief in myself. She was going to help me become
the person I wanted to be.

'This next week,' Sue went on, 'I want you to do something you've probably never done before. I want you to say no to your husband when he wants sex. At the moment, you're having sex with him whenever he wants, but you're arguing and he is not treating you the way you deserve to be treated. So you need to stand up for yourself and say no. Are you able to do that?'

'I'll try,' I replied doubtfully. I had never said no to Kieran before.

That night, after I put the kids to bed, I went about my normal routine of putting away the washing, tidying up the kitchen and getting ready for bed. Kieran and I hadn't been speaking much, although we weren't arguing either, so at least the house was peaceful. Kieran was watching TV, so I thought it was a good opportunity to get into bed before him. Maybe he would stay up for a bit and I could go to sleep and avoid having to say no to sex. I had only been in bed for half an hour or so when he came into the room, pulled back the sheets and lay down next to me. I was facing away from him and as I felt his leg come up over mine my heart began to race. *You need to say no, say no, you can do it*, were the words racing through my mind. It took every bit of strength in me to say that one word, that one single word that would give me back the power I needed to feel good about myself again. I finally opened my mouth. 'No, please don't,' I said, in somewhat of a pleading tone.

'What do you mean, no?'

I can't blame Kieran for wondering why, for the first time in our ten-year marriage, I was saying no to sex, but I couldn't go there, not until we were close again. With each new argument the distance between us grew. I was always keen to talk about our arguments to try to resolve them, but Kieran's response was to leave the house, walk for a few hours, then come home and pretend everything was okay. I knew each argument only added to the anger and resentment between us. That's why our disagreements were becoming more aggressive, more verbally abusive, because the resentment would rear up from the last unresolved fight.

That night was the beginning of something positive for me. It was the night I realised I could say no, and it actually felt good.

When I got up the next morning I wasn't surprised to find a note from Kieran saying he would be out for the whole day. That afternoon, after doing the shopping and picking up Josh and Jem from kindy, I made my way in the front door with an armload of grocery bags. Music was blaring from the living room. Not wanting to spark another argument with Kieran, I did not ask him to turn it down—that usually resulted in him accusing me of being controlling. I dropped the shopping in the kitchen and asked the boys to put away their bags before afternoon tea. 'What did you get up to today?' I called to Kieran as I walked past the living room. There was no reply. If Kieran didn't want to talk to me, he wouldn't. Walking into the bedroom to put my bag away, I noticed Kieran's side table was empty; his clock and book had gone. I checked the wardrobe: his clothes were gone too.

I walked into the living room. 'Where are all your things, Kieran? Are you going somewhere?'

'No,' he said abruptly. 'I have moved into the spare room and will stay there until you sort yourself out.'

'What do you mean, sort myself out? What have I done?'

'I know it's that woman counsellor's idea, that you use sex to emotionally blackmail me into getting what you want. Well, I won't stand for it,' he said, getting up off the lounge and leaving the room.

Emotionally blackmailing him? How could he see it like that? This was the first time I had ever tried to stand up for myself, to protect myself from getting hurt, and he saw it as emotional blackmail.

Kieran seemed to enjoy living in the spare room, and would often sing and dance around the house, without a care in the world. That annoyed me. How could he be so happy when there was so much distance between us? One night, I gave in. I seduced him back into the bedroom. That was the one thing I felt able to do, and I knew it would bridge some of the distance between us.

Still, the arguing continued. I knew our fights were damaging our boys. Something had to change. In a final attempt to save our marriage, we decided to move back to Brisbane. Maybe we could rebuild our marriage if we started going back to our old church, somewhere familiar where we had good friends. It was worth a try.

Chapter Sixteen

For the first time in many months I was happy and optimistic about our future. It felt good to be back in Brisbane. We had rented a house with a big yard and enrolled Josh in a local school. Kieran and I had stopped arguing and were getting on really well. With all the counselling and journalling I had been doing, I was beginning to feel free of the chains binding me to the past. I finally felt free to be me, although I was still learning who 'me' was.

On our first Sunday we were keen to return to the Gateway Baptist church. I didn't know it when we arrived, but it would be a memorable day. It felt good to be among friends and we had always loved Pastor Brian and his wife

Moira. They were a Kiwi couple who had previously pastored a small Baptist church in Mt Gravatt. It had grown so large they'd had to build a new church, which was Gateway. I loved Brian's messages from the pulpit; they were always down to earth and I felt inspired after his services.

As we stood up to sing at the end of the service, I felt washed with a deep peace. One of the pastors came to the microphone saying he wanted to give the opportunity for people who needed a touch from God to come forward. He said he thought there were a few people who needed special prayers. The worship leader started singing 'Amazing Grace', and a few people began walking towards the front. All of a sudden I was overcome by an intense feeling of sadness. What was happening to me? How could I go from feeling such peace to feeling as though I was losing control? My legs began to shake and tears flowed freely down my cheeks. It was then I knew I needed to go up the front. I had no idea why, I just knew I needed to.

It was a long walk down the aisle, but I didn't feel embarrassed. We all need prayer at different times of our lives. I was still nervous, though. I was relieved to see Corrine, one of the female pastors of the church, come towards me as I reached the front. She put her hand on my shoulder and began to pray. I started to cry much harder; it felt as though the grief was coming from the pit of my stomach. I was wailing like some people do at a funeral when they are struggling with unbearable loss. I couldn't understand what was going on.

All of a sudden, with my eyes closed, I could see a little girl. She was alone on a street corner and she was crying. I knew straightaway that the little girl was me, the six year old who had just been assaulted. I couldn't stop crying, the pain was so deep. Why was I hurting so much? I'd had counselling about this; I thought I had dealt with it. So why was it still causing me such anguish?

Out of nowhere I saw a huge blackboard with two words written on it in large white letters: *Forgive him*. What did that mean? I had been for counselling; didn't that mean I'd resolved this? The picture came again, *Forgive him*, and then a small voice seemed to speak to me from within: 'You need to speak it aloud.'

I was exhausted with the crying but the release of the emotion seemed to be calming me. I opened my eyes and said aloud to the man who had assaulted me, 'I forgive you.' At that moment it was like a huge weight had been lifted from my shoulders. By forgiving him I was freeing myself from the hold he had over me and I was finally free to move on. I had finally let go of the pain and let go of the man responsible for that pain. I was finally free of him.

That wasn't all that happened that day. I closed my eyes again and began to thank God for what he had just done in my life. I immediately saw another image, the same one I had seen years earlier of the heart pierced by arrows. This time, though, the picture was different. I could now see three arrows on the ground and three scars on the heart. I remembered then the image I'd had after I had forgiven Mum, with the one arrow on the ground and the scar. I saw the second arrow as representing my relationship with my dad. A few years before, after a day in tears journalling about Dad, about never having felt loved by him, about being a shadow in the background of his life and his never noticing me, I had talked with my counsellor. She had helped me to understand what my pain was all about and I freely forgave Dad at the time. I realised that my pain was due to my lack of self-esteem and self-respect. It was as if I was being the person that other people wanted me to be rather than the person I really was. The third arrow was the man who assaulted me.

There was still one arrow left in my heart, though. Where had this one come from and who did it belong to? Another season would come, I knew.

•

Despite all this wonderful healing I was experiencing, Kieran and I started to argue again. We sought the help of one of the pastors at church and he gave us counselling, so I was hopeful we would have a breakthrough in our relationship soon. This was not to be the case; in fact, the opposite happened. There was so much distance between us now that I felt as though I didn't even know this man anymore. It was as if he was living behind a huge wall, a wall I could not see over.

We had been to talk to the pastor again. It was my day off—I was working for another Avis franchise because Kieran was unemployed—and Kieran asked me to sit down because he wanted to talk to me about something. That morning the counsellor had brought up Kieran's attitude towards my brother Patrick. Kieran seemed to have taken a disliking to him and I was never sure why. Anyway, I sat down on the lounge chair opposite Kieran as he began to ask questions. 'Why do you think I don't like Patrick? What are you basing this accusation on?'

I was stunned by the line of questioning. Kieran got up to go to the bathroom, when he moved I saw a small red light flashing from under the cushion on his chair. I leaned forward to have a closer look and there, under the cushion was a small dictaphone that was on record. Before Kieran came back into the room, I quickly took out the tape and hid it in my sock.

'What have you been doing?' he shouted when he returned and noticed the cushion had been moved.

'What do you mean, what am I doing? What are *you* doing?' I replied. 'Why are you recording our conversation?' In the past I would never have challenged him like this, and I could tell he was surprised.

He seemed angry. 'In one of our sessions with the counsellor, he said it would be good if he had a recording of our conversations, so he really knew what was going on. That is why I am recording this, so he'll know the real truth. Give the tape back to me now!' he yelled.

I ran into the kitchen. 'I am not giving it back. This is an invasion of our home, an invasion of my privacy.'

'I swear I'll make your life difficult until you give it back!' Kieran shouted from the living room.

I couldn't believe what was happening. My husband of ten years was threatening me over a small cassette and a conversation we had had just moments earlier. I was later to discover he had previously taped our conversation twice, and was busy editing these conversations as 'evidence' of my controlling nature before he was going to hand them to our counsellor. I truly believe that Kieran thought he was doing the right thing and, like all relationship breakdowns, there are always two sides to the story. For me, I knew in my heart there was no way back from this. It was the beginning of the end.

That night Kieran slept in the spare room. I went to bed with my socks on, the tape still hidden there. I knew he wouldn't find it if he came looking in the middle of the night.

The next morning I had a doctor's appointment and needed to confirm the time. Josh and Jem were eating breakfast and I went to pick up the phone, only to find it was missing from the wall. 'Do you know where the phone is?' I asked the boys. 'Have you been playing with it?'

'No,' said Josh. 'I think Dad took it.'

Kieran was in his room. 'Where's the phone?' I asked, peering around the half-shut door. There was no reply. I thought I might as well forget trying to call and just show up at the surgery. I went to my bedroom to get my bag. I was sure I'd left it on the floor, but it was nowhere to be seen.

I went back to the kitchen to look there, and Kieran appeared. 'I'm taking the boys to school today,' he said, brushing past me.

'But I have a doctor's appointment,' I said quietly, trying not to alert the kids to the tension.

'You'll have to go another day,' he said quietly, and then called, 'Come on, boys, Daddy is taking you to school today.'

I gave Josh and Jem a kiss goodbye and watched as they left the house. I had realised by now that Kieran had taken my bag with the wallet and pulled the phone off the wall. I couldn't call anyone. Then it dawned on me that he had deadlocked both front and back doors as he left. I was horrified. I couldn't get out! I couldn't climb out of the windows, because they had security stays that limited the distance they could open. I was beginning to feel afraid. This was a man I didn't recognise. In the past we'd have our fights, he would walk out, come back hours later and we'd muddle on. This was different. He had never behaved quite like this, and I was afraid.

I sat on the edge of the couch, waiting for him to come home, determined not to let him intimidate me. Somehow I knew I needed to maintain a sense of calm. Kieran arrived home, deadlocking the door behind him. He didn't say anything, just went straight to his room. I got up and went to my bedroom; eventually I heard him unlocking the front door. I peered from behind the curtain and saw he was checking the mailbox. He came back in and closed the door behind him.

'Where are you?' he shouted. 'Are you inside?'

He must have thought I had escaped when he checked the mailbox.

He ran to the front door, then began running around the outside of the house screaming, 'Where are you?'

I was really scared now. I ran into Jem's room to hide. I stood as still as I could behind his bedroom door. Kieran came back into the house, still yelling, 'Where are you?' He went from room to room, searching. He arrived at Jem's door. My heart was beating so fast I was sure he would hear it. I was petrified. He threw back the door but still had a grip on the handle, so it only just touched my shoes. By some miracle he didn't see me.

He ran back outside onto the street and I heard the car engine revving. The car sped off up over the hill. My heart slowed a little, but I was still afraid. I didn't know what to do and I began to cry. 'God, what am I going to do? Help me, I'm scared.' A few minutes later, a car door slammed and Kieran came round the back of the house. I could see he was still mad, and I saw him kick a rock in the garden.

I remembered he hadn't locked the front door when he had run out to the car. If I could get to the car, I could escape! Our old Holden HQ had an ignition that could be started without the key.

I ran to the front door, trying to be as quiet as I could. I was guessing that he thought I wasn't home, which was why he'd come round the back. I ran out the front gate and jumped in the car. I began turning the ignition over; the car sounded like it wanted to start but it wouldn't catch.

I was shaking by now. I was desperate. 'Please start, please start,' I kept praying. I looked up and saw Kieran coming towards me, laughing. He had something in his hand. 'Did you want this?' he shouted. It was the distributor cap. My heart sank.

I got out of the car and began walking back towards the house.

'You can have the distributor cap and the car and your wallet, if you give me the tape!' said Kieran.

I couldn't fight any more. I was emotionally exhausted and just wanted it all to end. 'Fine! Have your stupid tape,' I said, retrieving it from my sock and throwing it at him.

Kieran followed me into the house and put my wallet and keys on the table. 'See, now, that wasn't so hard, was it?' He was triumphant. He had got his way. 'I'll even put the distributor cap back in the car for you,' he gloated.

He thought he had won. But he had lost me.

He went out and put the cap back on the car, then disappeared out the back to his shed. It was a room attached to the back of the house that Kieran had claimed as his own. I was never really sure what he did out there, apart from listen to music.

Picking up my keys and wallet I went for a drive. I decided to call the counsellor; perhaps he could help. I stopped at a phone box. I broke down as soon as the counsellor answered and I told him everything that had happened. 'I can't live with Kieran like this, something has to change.'

'Okay Stella, I'll see what we can do. Just try and stay calm for the boys and we will sort something out. I'll call you this afternoon. I think we may need to visit.'

I felt numb as I picked up the boys from school. 'How was your day?' I asked, smiling as they hopped in the car. There was no way I would let on to the boys that something was wrong. 'Hey, would you like to go for an ice cream?' The boys were thrilled, but I was only trying to delay going home, gathering my strength for what lay ahead.

When we arrived home Kieran was in his shed. The phone rang. It was the counsellor, Robert, who said he felt it would be best if he came over to talk to us both. He had a few things to do first, but he'd be here by seven-thirty. I felt relief wash over me. I wasn't alone with this.

Going out to the clothes line to bring in the washing, I poked my head in the door of the shed. I was nervous and a little scared of how Kieran would react. 'Robert, the counsellor, is coming over tonight to see us,' I told him.

Kieran gave me a blank look. 'What for?'

'Because I rang and told him what happened today he now wants to come and see us.'

'What time is he coming?' Kieran asked. I told him. 'Fine, I'll be in then,' he said.

I wasn't hungry at all and certainly didn't feel like cooking for Kieran, so I made a pot of pasta and sauce for the kids. I really wanted them in bed by the time Robert arrived. They had endured enough already. I didn't want them to hear tonight's discussion.

Robert arrived right on time. It felt as though someone had come to rescue me. 'Are you okay?' he asked, with a look of care and concern.

'I'm okay now,' I told him, 'but I was scared today.'

I showed Robert to the living room and went to call Kieran from the open back door. There was no reply from the shed. I knew he was in there as I could see his silhouette through the curtain. I went back inside and started boiling the kettle for a coffee.

Kieran came in a few minutes later, looking a little reserved. We talked for a while, then Robert said, 'I think it might be a good idea for you to spend time apart.'

'Okay then,' Kieran said.

I was surprised how quickly he agreed to it, but looking back, I can see he was probably as relieved as I was. We were both sick of the arguing. Nothing was said of the day's events, it wasn't necessary. After Robert left, I felt that a huge weight had lifted from my shoulders. I was going to be free for a while, free from the constant arguments we had been having.

Chapter Seventeen

The next morning, Kieran came into the kitchen with a duffel bag over his shoulder. He walked straight up to Josh and Jem, who were sitting at the table eating breakfast. 'Daddy is going to stay somewhere else for a while, but I'll come and see you as often as I can,' he said, leaning over to kiss them both on the head.

My heart sank. I had been hoping that Kieran and I would discuss how we were going to explain this to the boys and then tell them together.

'What do you mean, Daddy? Where are you going?' Josh asked, tears starting to trickle down his cheeks.

'Your mum and I are going to live apart for a while, but I'll still see you and you can come and stay with me.'

'But why? Have we done something wrong? I promise to be good, please don't go,' cried Josh. Jem sat motionless and silent, as though he was in shock. My heart broke seeing my poor little boys watch their dad leave.

Kieran had promised he would see the boys really soon. I knew he would. Kieran loved his boys so much.

When I heard the front gate shut, I picked Jem up in my arms and asked Josh to follow us into the living room. 'Mummy, what's wrong? Why has Daddy left us?' It was one of the hardest conversations I've ever had with my boys.

I sat them on the lounge, one on either side of me, and hugged them tight. 'You know how your mum and dad have been fighting a lot lately?' They solemnly nodded their little heads. 'Well, it's not good for us to argue like that. I know you boys have heard a lot of our arguments, and that is not good for you, so Mummy and Daddy are going to talk to someone about it. After we do that, everything should be okay.'

As I was telling them this, I felt as though I was just trying to console them. I really didn't know what was going to happen, whether Kieran and I would get back together. Right then, I guess I only wanted to give my boys hope. And because I had faith in God that our marriage could be saved. That hope didn't last long.

•

Kieran moved into the local caravan park so he could see the boys every weekend. After their visits with him, the boys would come home full of all the fun things they'd done. I was happy for them, but sad we couldn't be together as a family.

Kieran had taken the car when he left, so getting around was a problem. A couple of weeks after he left I opened a letter from Rebecca and out fell a cheque for a thousand dollars! Rebecca had heard from Mum that I was carless and she wanted to help. I was so excited and so thankful. I immediately started looking in the local classifieds. I was finally going to get my own car. The excitement was shortly to turn to absolute terror.

The very next day I spotted an ad for a 1987 Ford Laser, white, with low kilometres, no damage and only a thousand dollars. It was in a neighbouring suburb, so I rang straightaway and organised to see it the next day, a Saturday. Josh was at a friend's for the weekend, so only Jem was with me. I met the owner, Mark, and had a quick look over the car; it was old but in good condition. Mark said we could go for a test drive. The car was low on fuel, so he would drive to the service station at the end of the street to fill it up and I could drive from there. I put Jem in the back seat and clipped in the slightly loose seatbelt before jumping in the front and doing up my seatbelt as Mark began reversing down the driveway.

He pulled out onto the street and headed towards the service station. He slowed at a pedestrian crossing outside a small local supermarket to let an old lady cross the road. She was directly in front of the car when suddenly we heard a loud screeching of tyres. It seemed to happen in slow motion: the screeching of tyres, swinging my head around to try to see where the noise was coming from, and Mark stretching his arm across me to try to protect me. We were hit from behind with an almighty crash. Glass shattered everywhere. The poor elderly woman was thrown onto the bonnet, then disappeared. My seatback snapped on impact, but Mark had braced me, so I jerked backward then forward.

I heard screaming. It was Jem. 'Mum help me! Mum, Mum help!' I turned around to see my son covered in blood, a huge hole in his head above his eye. The impact of the 4WD sent my seat snapping backwards, with Jem's head connecting with the headrest as he was thrown forward. I could see the bone. I started screaming, 'Help, help, someone HELP!'

Within seconds there were people everywhere, coming out of houses and the supermarket. They helped me out of the car, onto the grass verge. 'My son! Please get my son!' I was hysterical. The rescuers were carefully assessing how to get Jem out of the car. They couldn't open the rear doors because they had been wedged shut by the impact. To reach through from the front could cause Jem further injury. Somehow they managed to get a crowbar and prise open the back door. It seemed to take forever. I was screaming and crying. Finally, they lifted him out and placed him gently on the ground next to me, his head on my lap.

He was now vomiting blood. Miraculously, an off-duty ambulance officer had been in the supermarket when the accident happened. 'Quickly, we need to turn him so he doesn't choke,' he said, and they gently turned Jem on his side. 'You need to stay calm. Try and breathe slowly. You need to stay calm for your son,' he said in a caring but strong voice. 'The ambulance will be here soon.'

I wanted to scream at him, 'My son is bleeding. He could be dying. I can't be calm!' But I knew he was right, that Jem needed me to be calm and reassure him it would be okay.

There were two young men standing nearby. 'My god, my god, I'm so sorry,' one of them kept saying. He seemed very young. I was later to find out he was just seventeen years old, on his learner's permit, driving his dad's big four-wheel drive. They had had the radio blaring and he had only seen us metres before he hit the brakes. The old lady we had stopped for was lying on the grass, being attended to by a nurse who lived in the street. The lady had broken her leg and I could see she was in pain.

Two ambulances arrived, one to transport Jem to the hospital and the other for the elderly lady. The paramedics worked quickly, checking Jem's vital signs and placing him on a stretcher. I rode with him in the back, holding his hand, reassuring him until we got to the hospital. They took him into surgery a couple of hours later. He had twelve internal and eighteen external stitches to his head, a few to his arm, and had several cuts and bruises to his face and body, but he was alive.

Jem had always had a dry sense of humour, beyond his years, and after the surgery I was allowed in to see him. I leaned over to give him a hug and he said with a grin, 'I guess that means we won't be buying that car, will we, Mum?'

I laughed. My beautiful boy was going to be okay. But the trauma of the accident stayed with me for a long time. The images of it are still with me today, sneaking up at random times and reminding me of what a precious gift my Jem is.

Chapter Eighteen

Adjusting to single life had its ups and downs. It was frantic at times, but there was a peace at home for the first time in a long while. The boys seemed to be more settled, so I knew it was right for Kieran and me to be apart. I had met a lovely couple through church, Alan and Edna. After the separation I found myself spending more time with them. They were like a rock for me. I would pop round for a coffee and they would offer me great support and advice. I also had a strong network of friends and would often meet girlfriends for lunch while the boys were at school. I was doing okay.

One Sunday night after the boys came home from a weekend visit with their dad, I was going about my usual routine, feeding the boys dinner, bathing them and getting them ready for bed. Tucking them in, I left them to settle, saying I would be in to kiss them goodnight in a minute. I was cleaning up in the kitchen when I heard a noise. It sounded like crying. I hurried back down the hall and found Josh lying in bed, sobbing into his pillow. 'Darling, what's wrong? Why are you crying?' I thought he was probably upset about saying goodbye to his daddy, so I wasn't prepared for what he said next.

'I don't want you to be sad, Mummy, but when I got up this morning there was a lady in Daddy's bed.'

It's hard to describe how I felt right then. Shocked, of course, but also defeated. But Josh was my concern in that moment; I was an adult and could deal with the pain later. 'Josh,' I said, stopping the tears I could feel welling up, 'my poor wee boy, I'm so sorry you had to see that.' What more could I say, how could I explain this? What could I say to my gorgeous eight-year-old son to make him feel better? There was nothing except, 'It'll be okay. Mummy loves you.' I held him tight for a few more minutes until he stopped crying. After he fell asleep I tucked him in, kissing him on the forehead, and quietly left the room.

I felt numb. What was I to do with this information? The very thought of my husband in bed with another woman made me feel sick. I went into the kitchen and opened the fridge. I had bought a cask of white wine a couple of days before and would have one or two glasses a night, finding it helped me sleep. I grabbed the cask and put it on the bench, filling the glass to the very top. The wine didn't touch the sides as I gulped it down like a glass of cordial. I wanted to erase the thoughts running around in my head.

I took the cask of wine to the couch. It seemed as if my whole world had just fallen apart. Who was she? What did she look like? How had he met her? Had he been seeing her for a long time? Why had I had been so naive as not to suspect this? So many questions were running through my mind. My heart hurt and I couldn't stop crying. I continued drinking until the early hours until the wine did its job of numbing the pain, then I fell into bed with my clothes still on.

I woke up to my alarm at 6 am, feeling as if I had been hit by a bus. My head and heart hurt, but I had two small boys to look after and I didn't want them seeing me like this. I had a shower and got myself ready for the day. Although I still felt incredibly sad, I somehow kept it all together. I had to, for Josh and Jem's sake.

I dropped the boys off at school and went straight to Alan and Edna's. I needed someone to talk to, someone to tell. I needed the help of someone who cared. After a couple of hours, a few coffees and a whole lot of tears, I felt so much better just having spoken about it.

The following week, Kieran arrived to collect the boys, as arranged. I heard the knock on the door and my heart began beating fast. I wanted to find out what was going on, but I wasn't sure how to approach the issue. Kieran was unpredictable and I could never be sure how he would react.

'Daddy's here,' I called out to Josh and Jem. 'Go grab your things. I just want to talk to Daddy about something.' I opened the door. Kieran's smile immediately turned to a frown.

'What do you want?' he demanded. I hardly ever went to the door. Kieran and I hadn't even spoken since he'd left. He was still blaming me for everything and I was avoiding him.

'I need to ask you something,' I said in a sheepish tone.

'I don't want to talk to you. I'm here to pick up the boys, where are they?' He turned to leave. 'I'll wait for them in the car.' That was it. I had no answers, couldn't even ask any questions. I kissed the boys goodbye, saying I loved them and hoped they would have a good time.

I went into the bedroom, sat down on my bed and picked up my journal. I needed to write my feelings down, to understand what was going on inside. Part of me just wanted to get mad, to get back at him, but the other part of me knew that anger and bitterness would change me, perhaps even ruin me. The only way I knew how to calm myself was to write it all out.

•

I decided I needed to create an opportunity to talk to Kieran. I called and suggested he might want some of our furniture. We didn't have much, but I knew he had moved from the caravan park to a small granny flat, and a few bits and pieces were sure to come in handy. Our conversation was brief. I told him the pieces I thought he might want and he said, 'I'll be around later today to get them.'

At around 7 pm a white van pulled up outside. Josh ran to the window. 'Yay, Jem, Dad is here!' He was excited and ran to open the front door. I saw Kieran approaching, but he wasn't alone, there was a woman walking behind him. I whispered to Josh, 'Is that the lady your dad was with last week?' He nodded and I suddenly felt sick—how could he bring this woman into the house? I was hurt and then I got angry.

He walked in, giving the boys a big hug. He didn't even look at me, let alone say anything. He just began picking up furniture and carrying it out of the house.

I was in shock. How was I supposed to talk to him now? He was in and out, moving things to the van, and had just about finished by the time I found the courage to approach him. 'Can I have a word with you in the kitchen,' I said quietly.

'What do you want?' he said angrily.

He followed me to the kitchen and I faced him, coming straight out with it. 'Are you having sex with her?'

'Mind your own fucking business!' he shouted. 'I don't have to tell you anything. Get out of my face.' He stormed past me to the front door. 'Come on, let's get out of here.'

And he left. I put the kids in the car and drove down the street to buy a packet of cigarettes. I held it together until I put the boys to bed. They had missed the exchange between their father and me and didn't seem unsettled by the day's events. I tucked them in, kissed them goodnight and went immediately to the fridge. I grabbed the cask and my new packet of cigarettes and went out to the back porch. Wasting no time, I poured the wine, lit the ciggie, finished them both in record time and repeated the exercise all night. Smoking was a way of dealing with stress for me and had been since I was thirteen. It had been a real struggle to give it up, but I had finally managed to do it when I fell pregnant with Josh.

My marriage is over, I realised with horror. I had my boys, but I was on my own. Kieran wasn't coming back. He had made it clear the way he looked at me and spoke to me that he was not interested in a reconciliation, regardless of whether he did or didn't sleep with that woman. I had to take control of our lives now, and that meant finding a new place to live. This house was full of sad memories. I wanted to escape as soon as I could.

The boys were beginning to show signs of being upset after some of the visits they had with their dad. I could always tell when Josh was angry he was only hiding his pain, so I needed to handle him with care. Don't get me wrong here, I certainly wasn't the perfect mother. I said and did things I had to say sorry for over the years and wished

I could take back, but we all make mistakes and I learned how to forgive myself too.

Josh had been out with his dad one day and was obviously upset when they got back. It wasn't long before he was arguing with Jem and I sent him to his room. When I went in to check how he was, Josh was tearing up a hat. 'Josh, what are you doing?' I said, grabbing the hat from him. Josh hated it when I was mad at him; he has a gentle spirit. He burst into tears. 'What's wrong? Did Dad get mad at you?' I asked, putting my arms around him to comfort him.

'No,' he sobbed. I held him until he stopped, but he didn't want to talk about it, and only wanted to be left alone. I didn't want to do that when he was so sad, but I did as he asked. I went straight to my room and began journalling. How could I reach Josh? How could I get him to share what was in his heart? It was as though a light was suddenly switched on: *That's it,* I thought. *I'll ask him to write it down for me, or draw it in a picture.*

I went back to his room to find him sitting dejectedly on his bed. 'If you can't tell me how you feel, do you think you might be able to write it down in a letter?' I asked.

'I'll try,' he said.

Five minutes later, I returned and Josh was crying again, but he handed me a piece of paper. This is what he wrote:

Dear Mum, These are my emotions of today expecaly [sic] about the hat with dad. I feel like I have to act like him to

> *be exepted [sic] like if he said there's a pretty lady I would*
> *have to say the same thing so it's quiet [sic] complicated to*
> *show you my emotions. I hope you understand, Love, Josh*

I understood why he had torn the hat; he wasn't angry, he was sad, and now I knew why. I had discovered a way I could communicate with the boys and I was to learn a lot from them in this way over the years.

Chapter Nineteen

Over the next couple of days, I filled my friends in on my decision and asked them to let me know of any properties coming up for rent. Lyn rang me. She had moved into a townhouse in a neighbouring suburb, and the two-bedroom unit opposite hers was available.

We made an appointment to look at it the following Saturday. It was perfect. It was part of a gated complex with a heated swimming pool. The unit itself was open-plan with the bedrooms and two bathrooms upstairs. It even had a small private courtyard. Our application was accepted a few days later. This was the beginning of our new life!

My wonderful church friends helped me pack up and clean the old house. They turned up on the Saturday before the move; one friend had made a meal for me, another had baked a cake, and their husbands brought their gardening equipment to mow the lawns, trim the overgrown hedges and clear out the back shed. I was totally blown away: by the end of the day, not only was most of the house packed, but the entire yard had been manicured as if by professional landscapers. I was overwhelmed by how kind everyone had been, and deeply grateful.

The following Saturday was moving day, and once again my friends came to the rescue. One arrived with a truck, and the men loaded while the women helped me do the last-minute packing and final clean. We were all pretty tired, but by 5.30 that afternoon my furniture was in the unit and I was standing in my new living room. I could hardly believe it. The boys were with Kieran again, so I was able to spend the night sorting the kitchen and making up their room. When they were dropped off the next afternoon, I wanted everything to feel like home.

Today was the beginning of a new life, were the first words I wrote in my journal the next morning. I was sitting in the sun in the little courtyard, sipping on a hot coffee. I knew this was where I could leave the old me behind and move on.

It was so good to see the boys later that day. 'Can we go for a swim, Mummy?' They were excited, running up the stairs to check out their new room.

'Of course you can.' It was only 5 pm and still warm, so we spent the next hour down at the pool. It was wonderful to watch them having fun. They had been through so much and it was good to see them laughing and splashing about in the water. It had only been a day, but I knew I had done the right thing—we were home.

The boys' visits with Kieran were going well. He would usually have them every second weekend, sometimes more often. There had only been an occasional time when he'd phoned to cancel. One Sunday, however, I could see that the visit had not gone well. Josh and Jem were unusually subdued and their clothes were filthy.

I hugged them at the door. 'How was your weekend? Did you have fun?'

Josh just looked at the floor and Jem slowly wandered up the stairs to his room.

'What's wrong, Josh? Your clothes are dirty and you don't seem very happy.' I sat him down on the couch and put my arm around him.

'I didn't like it this time. We didn't stay at Dad's house, because when we got there, there was a police car and all Dad's stuff was out on the lawn.' He was staring at the floor in a kind of daze.

I sat him on my lap and hugged him. 'You poor boys, that must have been horrible. What happened then, where did you go?' I was trying to stay calm, not wanting Josh to know how much my mind and heart were beginning to race.

'Dad took us to this house. I didn't know the people, and I didn't want to stay there, but Dad said it would be okay.' I held my breath, wondering what else my poor boy was about to say. 'It was a really dirty house and all they did was smoke. Jem and I had to stay in a room that had rude pictures on the walls. We had to share a bed with dirty sheets. Daddy said we wouldn't stay the night, but we woke up there this morning. Jem didn't know where he was and started to cry, but I tried to make him feel better by saying we would be going home soon. I was scared, Mummy, and I don't want to go back there.'

I held him close, comforting him and reassuring him that he and Jem would never have to go back there again. I would make sure of that. I was mad. How could Kieran take them into that environment? They were only six and eight years old.

After dinner, I gave them a hot bath, put them into clean pyjamas and tucked them into bed. 'I'm so glad to be home, Mum,' Josh said.

'Me too,' said Jem.

'I'm glad you're home too. I love you both so much and I will look after you, I promise. You can see Daddy next weekend if you want to, but if you don't, that's okay, I can tell him.'

'I'd like to see him, but I don't want to go back to that house,' Josh said, and Jem nodded.

'Don't worry, I'll take care of it,' I said, leaning over to give them a kiss goodnight.

The next day, I was anxious to get in touch with Kieran's flatmate. It sounded as though Kieran had been thrown out. I was shocked when I heard what had happened. Apparently Kieran had started behaving irrationally, to the point where his flatmate had to ask him to leave. He wouldn't go, so finally the police had been called in to evict him by force.

Okay, now I had the information, how was I going to handle it from here? I had to speak to Kieran. What I had been told was making me doubt his ability to keep the boys safe. I knew Kieran loved his boys and I didn't want to stop him from seeing them, but they had to feel safe when they were with him.

I got his phone number from a friend and steeled myself to make the call. As soon as Kieran realised it was me on the phone, he was on the defensive. 'What do you want?'

'I need to know where you're living now. Josh said you're not living in the same place. I need to know that the boys will be somewhere safe this weekend,' I said, trembling inside.

He answered me coldly. 'They are my sons and it has nothing to do with you where I take them.'

Suddenly, for the first time, I felt a real strength. I was fighting for my boys. I had to protect them. I was scared to stand up to Kieran, but this was about Josh and Jem. I was calm as I said, 'Kieran, it has everything to do with me. If you don't have a place for them to sleep overnight, they can't stay with you. Why don't you take them for the day instead?'

'I don't want to talk to you.' He was shouting now. 'You can't tell me where I can or can't take my sons. I will be there to pick them up on Saturday!' He hung up the phone.

I was stunned at Kieran's reaction. When I got off the phone I rang the solicitor for advice. I needed to talk to someone. The solicitor said that under those conditions I couldn't let Kieran take Josh and Jem. He thought it would be wise to let Lyn, my neighbour, know in case the police needed to be called on Saturday.

I was anxious all week. I was going to have to confront Kieran and tell him he couldn't have the boys overnight. At ten on Saturday morning I heard the sound of his music blaring from the car radio. He had obviously followed a car into the compound to gain access. I usually sent the boys to the gate when he buzzed. I had asked Josh and Jem to stay in their room and had shut their door so they wouldn't hear too much.

I opened the front door to see Kieran getting out of the car. He was shirtless and had a beer in his hand. Things had certainly changed. He was obviously very upset that I had put restrictions on his visit with the boys. I really didn't want to stop him seeing them. I knew he loved them and they meant the world to him but I had to take a stand to protect them. 'Get out of my face,' Kieran sneered as he got out of the car and began making his way to the door. 'I am here to pick up my boys.'

'I told you,' Kieran, 'You can take them but not overnight unless you can tell me you have somewhere safe to take them. They don't want to go back to that house you took them to last week, they were scared.' He began moving toward the front door but I ran ahead of him and pulled the screen door shut behind me.

'I am taking my boys overnight, and I will rip the door off the fucking hinges to get them!' I understood him being angry but this behaviour was out of character for him. I had never seen Kieran react like this, he had so much hate in his eyes toward me. If only he knew all I was trying to do was protect his children. I never wanted to stop him seeing them. I knew he loved them but what I had learned the week before had changed everything. The situation was out of control and I knew things were going to get worse.

He was enraged and I was terrified. I was holding on as tight as I could to the screen door, praying, *Please God, don't let him in, please protect me and the boys.* Then suddenly he turned and walked back to the car. He sat on the bonnet and began calling out to the boys, 'Josh, Jem, Daddy is here. We're going to McDonald's. Come on, I'm waiting.'

He called out a few more times but it became obvious they weren't coming down. He came back to the screen door, which I had been able to lock, so I felt safer. 'I'll be back to get my boys. Mark my words, I'm coming back to get them!' He returned to the car, slammed the door and took off, the car screeching, leaving behind black tyre marks.

I took a deep, shaky breath. I was so relieved he had gone, but I was scared of what he might do. He seemed out of control with rage. I didn't recognise him; he certainly wasn't the man I had married.

The solicitor had suggested packing a few bags, just in case we needed to leave in a hurry, so I was prepared. I asked the boys to get into the car, saying we had to go away for a while. I could see their confusion. I knew they'd heard Kieran, but he was behaving in such an unfamiliar way, they couldn't make sense of what was going on. Who was this man? It wasn't the dad they knew and loved.

I grabbed the bags and went to a friend's house. From there I called the solicitor to let him know what had happened. He consulted with the pastors of the church and they decided it wasn't safe for the children and would be wise if we removed ourselves from the situation for a while. They booked and paid for a bus trip to Melbourne the following day. I trusted the pastors and left them to make the decision about what was the right thing to do. Looking back, it was all so surreal. One minute we were a couple separated by our differences and the next minute I was on a bus with our sons in the middle of the night running away from my husband. How was this happening?

In Melbourne I phoned Lyn to see if Kieran had returned. He had, parking the car on the side street and walking into the complex with a ghetto blaster blaring loud music. She told me he had banged on my front door for a long time, then crossed to her place to ask where I was. She said he didn't look well. He'd left Lyn's and approached the manager, demanding he tell him where I had gone. The manager had called the police, alarmed by his threatening behaviour. Before the police had arrived, Kieran had left a letter on my screen door. The police took the letter. Apparently it was threatening to me.

I was shocked to hear how much Kieran had changed, and I was grateful to be a long way away from him. We stayed with Rebecca for a couple of nights, but then found that Kieran was ringing around all of the people we knew in Melbourne. He had rightly assumed this was where we would go. We had to keep moving, in case he discovered where we were. Michael and Moira offered for us to stay with them. They were the couple who had rented their home to us when we left the halfway house. They had recently moved into a new home and Kieran would not know where they lived. They were a godsend; they lent us a car, and when Michael learned how little money I had, and the bills I still had to pay, he didn't hesitate to write out a cheque, clearing all the money owing. Michael was also great with the boys. He and Moira had two girls of similar ages, so the kids played together, but Michael made a real effort to make Josh and Jem feel special. It meant a lot, particularly after what they had been going through with Kieran. I will be forever grateful to Michael and Moira for making that part of my life easier with their generosity and kindness to us.

At the end of the second week, one of my friends phoned to say that Kieran had rung and he was planning to hitchhike down to Melbourne to find me. I knew I had to get some professional advice, so I rang our solicitor in Brisbane. He advised me to take out a protection order. I was stunned. How had our lives come to this, that I would have to take out an order to stop my boys' father from seeing us? But I was scared, and I knew I had to do whatever I could to protect us.

I went to the police station the next day. I had to attend court and give a full account of what had been happening. The judge stamped the order, which was valid for the next four weeks. However, it was only valid in Victoria. If I wanted to return home I would need to reapply in Queensland. With the boys I was always very honest. I tried to make it into an adventure for them but I didn't disguise what was going on.

I was living day to day, trying not to think about what was going to happen next. We had been in Melbourne for four weeks when I got a phone call to say Kieran had started living on the streets and had been arrested. It seemed Kieran wouldn't be coming to Melbourne, after all, so I knew this would be a good time to return with the boys to Brisbane. They had been out of school for long enough and needed some normality back in their lives. I would just have to face whatever happened when we got back. Home wasn't the unit, however. I no longer felt safe there. We would have to find another place to live. We stayed with friends and a week later moved into another unit. I applied for the Queensland protection order. I was still scared of what Kieran might do.

Looking back, it seems surreal. I felt as though I was living a nightmare that I couldn't wake from. It had happened so fast: one minute we were a normal couple with everyday issues that could be resolved by counselling, the next minute I was fleeing interstate with my children and taking out protection orders.

•

We settled into our new home and life slowly began to return to normal. I was keeping in touch with Kieran's friend, Steve. Josh and Jem were missing their dad, however, so I arranged for them to spend some time with him, so long as Steve stayed with them. They went for a day at the beach and seemed happy when they got home.

I rang Steve for an update. He told me that Kieran had undergone a psychiatric assessment. He had been diagnosed with bipolar disorder. All of a sudden, things started to make sense. In a way it was a relief to have an explanation for his behaviour, which was so out of character. With a diagnosis Kieran would be able to get the help he needed. The question remained whether or not he would agree to that, of course. We would just have to wait and see.

Chapter Twenty

The boys were back at school, we had made friends in the new unit block and we were getting on with living a new life. The boys hadn't seen their dad for months but they seemed to be adjusting. I had a new job working for Avis head office in sales. I had a lovely new company car and life was finally becoming normal for us.

I arrived home from work one day and received a phone call from one of the producers of *This Is Your Life*, a popular television program documenting the life of an Australian celebrity. They had chosen Rebecca and were researching her story. They wanted me to tell them a little about our experiences growing up. The show would be recorded the following month and they would be flying Mum and all us brothers and sisters to Sydney, putting us up at the same hotel, all expenses paid. I was so proud to know Rebecca was going to be honoured for all her hard work. I was excited too—the Gibney family was scattered between New Zealand and Australia, so chances for us all to be together were rare.

The weekend finally arrived. I had arranged for a friend to look after the boys and had dropped them off. Waiting for the taxi to pick me up, I was buzzing with excitement. The cab finally arrived with my big sister Teresa inside. She was as excited as I was; we felt like we were running away for a couple of days—no cares or responsibilities! Teresa was kept busy with six children and she lived on the other side of Brisbane, so we didn't see much of each other. We immediately started laughing and catching up.

In Sydney we were taken to the hotel where we joined up with the rest of the family. It was such a joy for all of us to be together. We're very close, even though we don't see each other often, and when we're together there's always the Gibney magic. We had dinner and met briefly with the crew and producers of *This Is Your Life* to get a rundown of the next day's events. Rebecca had no idea about what was going to take place. I felt rather special as I had been asked to help with what was called 'the sting'—when they surprised the unknowing guest. The next day I went with one of the producers to the Channel Nine studios. There I was introduced to Mike Munro, the host of the show, the camera crew and the photographer. *Oh gosh, you're cute!* I thought, as I was introduced to Paul, the photographer.

We spent some time going over how the sting was to take place. I was told all I needed to do was follow the crew, and when they said 'Now!' I was to step out from behind Mike, walk towards Rebecca and give her a hug. It all went smoothly, and Rebecca was taken completely by surprise. The secret had been kept well. We Gibneys are capable of keeping secrets, good and bad.

They took us back to the studio and ushered us into a private room to wait until it was time to record the studio segment. Rebecca was not allowed to see anybody, as all the guests were to be a surprise. I was called an hour or so after we got there to do a rundown during rehearsal. It was nerve-racking. I had never been on TV before. I was petrified! But I seemed to do okay. I only had a few lines, and it was over before I knew it, then it was back to the room to keep Rebecca company. The time came to record the show and we were taken to the set. Rebecca went out the front and I waited with the family. I was nervous, but walking out on that stage with all my brothers and sisters made it easier. It was a great night and Rebecca was overwhelmed by all of the guests they had brought together to honour her achievements.

After they stopped filming, we were all laughing and talking together. They had an after-party, where the guests were invited to have a few drinks and nibbles to celebrate. We fondly recalled the good times we had enjoyed and there was a great deal of laughter. We're incredibly close as a family and we've got a strong bond, which many people admire. Of course, Paul the photographer was there, snapping away. We started chatting, and we really hit it off. Everyone was having such a great time, we didn't call it a night until three in the morning!

The next day we were picked up by limo and taken out to Palm Beach. It was the most beautiful place I had ever seen, the ocean on one side and the calm waters of Pittwater estuary on the other. Rebecca's friends had lent her their holiday home overlooking the beach. The views were breathtaking. I loved standing at the water's edge, soaking up the feeling of calm. We spent the day together reminiscing about our lives as kids, while we drank champagne and ate gourmet food. It was one of the best days I could remember, and I didn't want it to end. By late afternoon, however, each of us had different directions to go in, different lives to get back to. I was sad to say goodbye but grateful we had had this special time. What I didn't realise as we drove away was that I would be back in the not-too-distant future. A new season was coming.

•

Back in Brisbane, I received a photo taken on the night of *This Is Your Life*. It was a family shot. I knew other pictures had been taken and I was interested to see them. I phoned Channel Nine and spoke with the publicity department. They gave me the phone number of the photographer. Of course it was Paul. I think in the back of my mind I had secretly been hoping I would get a chance to talk to him again. We had been so comfortable chatting that night. I was nervous as I dialled, but he answered the phone and recognised me straightaway. We immediately slipped back into a familiar friendship. At the end of the conversation, Paul asked if he could call me again. I was thrilled.

He rang me at the end of the week and we talked for at least a couple of hours. Before long, this was happening nightly. We didn't seem to run out of things to say, it was wonderful. We laughed and joked. I was on cloud nine as I hung up each night. He was a very kind and caring man, very laidback in his manner and lifestyle. One evening, Paul said, 'How about I come up and visit for a weekend?' I'd been hoping he'd suggest that! He flew up that weekend and we had a fabulous time. I introduced him to the boys and he was great with them. Of course the next thing that happened was me flying to Sydney to see him. Paul lived by the water at Palm Beach. Palm Beach! That wonderful place we had stayed when I flew to Sydney. It was just as gorgeous as I remembered. Before I knew it we were flying backwards and forwards and this thing with Paul was turning from friendship to something more serious. I hadn't heard from Kieran's friend for at least six months and I wondered whether Kieran would ever contact the boys again. The last I heard he was living on the streets of the Gold Coast, which was no place for Josh and Jem.

If this was to be a long-term relationship and I knew it could be, then it would be the right decision to move. But the boys were settled in school with good friends.

Paul had a good job and a beautiful place to live. My situation was a little different. I could see the Palm Beach lifestyle would be fantastic for two young boys, playing by the water, boating, snorkelling. And the water gave me a sense of calm every time I was near it. It seemed to be a no-brainer. But could the boys handle further upheaval?

I flew home, asking that question over and over in my head. I didn't want to be impulsive; I needed to do what was in the boys' best interests. By the time I got home I had decided that I would take them down with me on the next visit and let them decide. I also made a list of the doors that would have to open for us if we were to make the move. Number one: somewhere to live. The rent would have to be manageable, because the second door—work—would have to pay that rent. Door number three: where would the boys go to school? Of course none of this would be a problem if the boys didn't like Sydney. I prayed about it all, asking God to open those doors or shut them. It was up to Him.

I talked to the boys. They were excited to make the trip. They already had a good relationship with Paul. When I described Palm Beach to them, they couldn't wait to get to the water. Paul decided to fly up and drive down with us, so one weekend we all piled into the car and made our way south for a few days.

Paul lived on the water on the Pittwater side of Palm Beach, and the boys were excited when we arrived. They immediately tore down to the water's edge, fossicking around and exploring as boys do. I reminded God that I had those doors that needed opening. It all had to fall into place. First thing: accommodation. After a look through the local rental listings, I was a bit discouraged. The Northern Beaches was so pretty, everybody wanted to live there. There wasn't a lot on offer and it seemed pricey. I thought, *Okay, the property door is shut for now, let's go to door two.* I phoned the local Avis franchise, as I was working for them in Brisbane and I thought that might get me a favourable response. It did. Steve, the franchise manager, was very encouraging on the phone and we made an appointment for Monday.

On to door three: schooling. I had already looked on the internet and found a small Christian school in Terrey Hills, only thirty minutes' drive from Palm Beach. This would be a similar environment to the one the boys were used to in Brisbane. The school was easily accessible by car, but Palm Beach was also on the school bus route. I rang and was able to make an appointment for Monday. It was going to be a busy day.

On the Monday we all piled into the car and headed off to the school. We were met by the principal, who seemed sincere and easy to talk to. The boys loved the grounds of the school. I explained that I was a single mum and wouldn't be able to afford the full fees. 'We do have fee relief but it is determined on a case-by-case basis,' said the principal. 'We can only offer it to three families per year, so I will have to look into it and get back to you.' We would have to wait to hear whether this door would open for us.

Our next stop was at the Avis franchise. The interview was going well, but I was still surprised when, after only half an hour, Steve offered me a job. It sounded perfect. It was for three days a week as a sales executive, building relationships with local corporate clients. 'So when can you start?' Steve asked. I hadn't expected to be offered a job on the spot, and wasn't entirely sure I was even going to move, but I didn't let on. I knew this was the first door to open.

'It may not be until early next year. I need to confirm a place at the school I have found for the boys, but if it all goes to plan it will be before the school year starts in late January.' Steve seemed to think that was fine and we shook hands and said goodbye. I couldn't believe it, I had a job. I was nervous. Was I doing the right thing? But I kept reminding myself of the promise I had made to God. If this was the first door, He still had two more doors to open.

We made our way back to Brisbane, the boys excited about the possible move. I had no need to worry whether this would be good for them. The lifestyle they would have by the water would be amazing. I was still keeping things in check, however. The accommodation needed to be sorted and the schooling.

I didn't have long to wait. A few weeks passed and I received a phone call. The school board had granted me fee relief so my boys could attend next year. I was thrilled, but I didn't tell the boys because I wanted to wait for a house to come up.

A few weeks later, we were counting down the days till Christmas. I was beginning to let go of the idea of moving. Paul and I had both been looking at accommodation but it was all too expensive for me to afford on my new salary. I decided that if I had not heard anything by the end of the week, I would call the school to cancel and re-enrol them at their present school for the following year. The third door had not opened.

On the Thursday night, after putting the boys to bed, I called Paul. We spoke nearly every night, but I hadn't told him of my decision. I knew he would be as upset as I was. Paul sounded excited when he picked up the phone. 'I was about to call you, you must have read my mind! I got a call from a friend today. He has a house in Newport that he is going to rent out cheap. It's only for three months but it will give you time to get settled and keep looking. Being here will make it easier for you to find something.'

I couldn't believe it. The third door was opening. Thank you, God! Now I knew this was right for us! I was excited and couldn't wait to tell the boys the good news. We were moving to start a new life in Sydney!

Chapter Twenty-one

We arrived in Sydney in the January and moved into the house in Newport. It was small, but it had three bedrooms and a large deck overlooking Pittwater. The boys started school in the February and I began working in my new role at Avis in Dee Why that same week. We all loved living near the beach and would spend most of our time there. We were beginning to feel settled.

Our three-month rental period came to an end all too soon and the only place I could find within my price range was a flat on the main road in Palm Beach. It wasn't flash; it had mould growing in one of the bedrooms, and no heating, but I was going to try to make the best of it. After our first winter there, though, I decided we needed something warmer. I couldn't believe it when I discovered an apartment perched high on the hill in Palm Beach, with amazing views of Pittwater from nearly every room. It was the most beautiful apartment I had ever seen. It was fully furnished and looked like something out of a magazine. I fell instantly in love, I wanted to live there. The rent was of course much more than I was paying. It wasn't going to leave me much left over, but I didn't want to think about that, I just knew I wanted to live there. I had lived with second-hand things all my life, feeling like a second-class citizen; this was my chance to feel like everyone else. I threw caution to the wind and made the application. I had done the sums and knew it would be hard but manageable. It was such a great feeling taking all the old furniture I had bought from the op shops to the tip. I felt as though I was getting rid of my old life and starting a new one.

I loved our new home, and so did the boys. It was opposite the wharf on Palm Beach, and the boys would spend most of their spare time down on the water. They had made friends with a few local boys around the same age, and would often go swimming or snorkelling around the foreshore. They were happy, which made me happy.

We had only been living in our new apartment for a couple of weeks when I received a letter that took me back twenty-two years, to the day I gave my son up for adoption. It was a letter from the social welfare department in New Zealand stating that my son had been in contact with the department. He had received the letter I had sent to them some four years earlier. I had written to him on his nineteenth birthday. I wanted him to know the truth about why I had given him up, to let him know I was thinking about him, and that I thought about him often. I wanted to say I was sorry for giving him up. I knew that by law he wouldn't be in touch until he was 'of age', which would be when he was twenty, so he was very much on my mind.

Now he wanted to make contact with me! I was excited and terrified at the same time. Had he forgiven me? Did he understand the choice I'd made? What was he like? I had so many questions running through my mind. I replied to the letter immediately: I was happy for the social welfare department to pass on my contact details and would love to hear from him.

A couple of weeks later the letter arrived. It was from Corey, my firstborn son. I had named him Christopher but his adoptive parents had renamed him Corey. My hands were trembling as I opened the letter.

A few weeks and a couple of long, wonderful phone calls later, Corey made plans to come to Australia. I wanted to meet him at the airport by myself. I bought a single rose. I wanted to give him something that would tell him I loved him. I was so nervous as I stood waiting. A jumble of thoughts were racing through my mind. Would he like me? What did he look like? Would I recognise him? It seemed like hours later, but was probably only thirty minutes, when he finally walked through from Customs. I knew straightaway it was him because he closely resembled his dad. He was an exceptionally good-looking young man, with fair hair and a gentle demeanour. He was looking around the crowded terminal; he hadn't seen me yet. I walked towards him, holding out the red rose. He saw me and there was no hesitation, no awkwardness at all. We embraced immediately and both began to cry. We were oblivious of anyone around us. We were finally together and it felt wonderful. After twenty-two years of thinking about him, wondering if he was okay, if he was happy, here he was in my arms. I didn't want to let go, and I sensed he felt the same. It was a long while before we broke apart. That hug is a moment I will never forget.

On the drive back to Palm Beach we simply couldn't stop talking. He sounded like me in so many ways, the way he talked, his passion for life. He told me he loved playing the cornet and that he had brought it with him. I wanted to hear him play, so when we got home I drove around to the headland. It was a beautiful sunny day and there were lots of people about. We made our way to the park bench overlooking the ocean and Corey put the cornet to his lips and played the Last Post. It brought tears to my eyes as I sat there listening to my son play for me. Afterwards he tried to teach me, but I couldn't even blow a note. We laughed and cried all at the same time.

We made our way back home in time to meet Josh and Jem off the school bus. It was obvious they were brothers from their personalities, and they slipped into an easy relationship from the outset. They laughed at the same things and there was an instant connection between the three of them, which has been growing ever since. We spent the evening getting to know each other, talking nonstop and laughing. It was one of the most memorable weekends of my life, getting to know the man I had given away as a baby. The years of separation melted away; it was as though he had always been with us, part of the family. His personality is very similar to mine, but he is his own man. He's more reserved than me but he's got the same drive that I have and we understand each other.

A few years later as a family we flew to New Zealand to meet Corey's adoptive mother, Carol. She was a warm and kind woman and had been a great mum to Corey. Carol had shared with me in a letter how she'd felt when the son she had raised had told her he was going to meet his birth mum. She had been in agony inside, but understood his need to do it. I felt for her, reassuring her I had no intention of trying to take over her role as Corey's mum. She had been there for him all his life and I hadn't.

The day we met a year or so later, we sat for hours sharing our lives. Carol had made me a scrapbook of photos and memorabilia of Corey's life. She had filled in the gaps of all those years for me—what a special woman. She also had a poem for me that she had printed and framed, it was called 'The Legacy of an Adopted Child'.

We had a fabulous few days together. I will forever be grateful to Carol for welcoming me into their lives.

Looking back, I had always wondered whether I had done the right thing by adopting my son out. It wasn't until I met him years later that I realised he had a good life that I couldn't offer him when I was fifteen. Now I am very much at peace with this part of my life, but for many years I felt terribly responsible for giving him up. I needed to ask him for forgiveness, which he readily gave to me.

Corey is very much part of our family today and although he and his wife Sarah live in New Zealand and we don't get to see each other as often as we would like, when we do catch up, it's as though we've never been apart. The boys now have an older brother they love, I have three sons and a daughter-in-law.

Chapter Twenty-two

We had been in Sydney for over a year and still had no word from Kieran. I decided it was time to move on, time to cut the ties of my marriage. So I filed the divorce papers with my solicitor in Brisbane and then, after attending a hearing, and with no objections from Kieran, our marriage was over. We were divorced.

Paul wanted me to move in with him. The complex he was living in had a two-bedroom unit come up for rent. We were getting along well and had even discussed marriage, but I wasn't ready for that sort of commitment yet. I was thinking of the boys, and how it would impact on them. In the end, though, it seemed silly not to pool our resources.

We were spending most of our time together anyway, and Paul got on so well with Josh and Jem, so we took the leap, secured the unit and moved in together.

It was perfect for the four of us. It was right on the waterfront, and there was a little ladder leading down to the beach. In the evenings we would sit out on deckchairs watching the sun go down, sipping a glass of wine, a fishing line slung into the water. It was magic. The boys loved it; they would come home from school and go straight into the water, either swimming, snorkelling or spearfishing. Although I was sad for them that they didn't see their dad, they seemed happy and settled.

Paul and I had been living together for a few months when he proposed to me. I was over the moon. What more could I ask for? I had a man who loved me, two beautiful boys, a great job and a fabulous place to live. When I told the boys, Josh was happy for me. Jem was a little reserved; it would take him a bit more time to come around to the idea.

In front of our home was a big rock where we would all sit to watch the sunset, have a picnic or daydream. It was a special place for the four of us and Paul and I decided to be married there. It was a beautiful sunny day. I arrived by tinny (a small aluminium boat), driven by Paul's best man, Jim. He walked me from the wharf along the waterfront. My boys were waiting for me and, their arms linked through mine, they escorted me to Paul and the celebrant, who were waiting on the rock. Afterwards we had a supper and a wonderful evening with close friends and family, watching the sunset and celebrating. Paul and I were so happy, our future looked so good.

It was an ordinary day and I was just home from work, checking the mailbox on the way inside. There was a letter addressed to me that had the *Department of Legal Services* stamped on the outside. Immediately I felt nervous. I opened it to find a letter sent from the Legal Aid Department in Brisbane.

I was in shock. The letter stated I had left Queensland without Kieran's consent and had taken his children from him. In my naivety, I hadn't even considered this. I'd thought I was doing the best thing for all of us by moving to Sydney. Why would Kieran go through Legal Aid rather than call me? I had always wanted the boys to have a relationship with their dad; they loved him and wanted to see him although we had not heard from him for over a year and my solicitor had advised me to deny access until Kieran could prove he was able to provide a safe environment for the boys during access visits. What if he was well again now? Maybe it would be safe for the boys. I hoped so; they would be so happy to see their dad again.

After a telephone conference with a solicitor in Brisbane, a written legal agreement was drawn up. I was reassured by what I was told by Legal Aid in Brisbane about Kieran's living arrangements. The boys' safety was paramount in the agreement. Kieran was to have access every holidays, and he and I were to share the costs of the coach fare to and from the Gold Coast, where Kieran was living.

The boys were thrilled—they were to see their dad for two weeks in the Christmas holidays. A couple of weeks beforehand, Kieran rang to say he couldn't afford his portion of the coach fare and would have to cancel. I was furious. How could he let his boys down like this? I wasn't going to let Josh and Jem be disappointed, so I decided to pay the full fare. Paul thought it wasn't a good idea, that it wasn't part of the legal agreement, but even though I agreed with him, I couldn't bear to see my boys hurt any more.

They did go and see their dad in those holidays and the arrangement went reasonably well for a while afterwards. Then the calls started, cancelling, saying he couldn't afford the coach fares again. I knew I couldn't keep paying, and the visits dropped to two that year, and one the following year. The boys were hurt but I knew it wasn't right for me to make it happen every time.

•

Josh was not happy when he arrived home from school one day. I knew something was very wrong, but he wouldn't talk about it. What had happened to make him so withdrawn? I thought of all the things that could happen at school that might cause him to act like this. Someone must have said something to hurt him, or he must have got into trouble for something. I went to his room and asked him, 'What happened at school today? Was someone mean to you?'

'No,' he replied. 'We just had to draw a picture describing our life and I couldn't do that.'

I thought perhaps he hadn't felt safe, or he hadn't wanted to be vulnerable, letting everyone else know what was really happening on the inside. 'Can you draw it for me?' I asked. 'Maybe that might help.'

'I can try,' he replied.

After a few minutes he came out of his room and passed me a small piece of paper. I saw instantly the fragile nature of my son's heart. He had drawn a large man holding a tiny stick figure. Over the man's head he had written *Dad*. Over the tiny stick figure was *Me*. In the top left corner, there was a picture of a face with a speech bubble saying, *Come back*. Under this face he had written *God*.

I understood it straightaway. Josh had talked in the past of how he felt. By drawing himself in his dad's hands, he was showing how he was being controlled by him. To feel loved by his father, he had to like the things his dad liked, behave just like his dad behaved. He felt God was saying to him, 'Come back to who *you* are.' By seeing this so clearly in his drawing, Josh could work out how to get himself out of his father's (imaginary) clutch and be himself. He made a huge step forward that day. He was still in pain, but he could see why.

•

On another occasion I felt a distance between Jem and me. I was finding it hard getting close to him.

He seemed angry with me. I didn't know what I had done; every time I asked him what was wrong, he would fob me off, saying everything was fine. He came home from school one day and seemed sad. I suggested that if he couldn't tell me what was going on, or couldn't understand it himself, maybe he could try drawing a picture.

I wasn't prepared for what he drew. At the top it said 'You say friends aren't real', then there was an arrow underneath pointing to 'I believe it', then another arrow pointing to 'I get upset', then another arrow pointing to 'I resent you', then another arrow pointing to 'You get mad', then an arrow pointing right back up to the top, 'You say friends aren't real.' It represented a cycle of his feelings. It broke my heart to see it written in black and white, how I had hurt Jem. I put my arms around him. 'I am sorry, Jem. When did this happen? It didn't sound like something I would say. We talked and he reminded me of a day when he had come home from school upset at something that had happened with a friend. I think I must have said something along the lines of, 'Sometimes you find out who your real friends are.' Jem had taken it to heart, thinking I meant his friends weren't his real friends. I was appalled. I always tried to communicate really clearly with the boys; they had such a lot to deal with in life. This time I must have been busy, or distracted. I had obviously hurt my son without realising. What we say and what someone hears can be two different things. This had sent Jem off on a path of questioning his choice of friends and made him doubt them. I felt really disappointed in myself. I cried with him, apologising for the pain I had caused him. He forgave me that day and I learned a valuable lesson—to be very careful what I said to my sons.

Chapter Twenty-three

I had been working at Avis since I had arrived in Sydney. It was a good job and I had made a great friend in Shelley. She worked as a rental sales agent, and we had lots of laughs and chat sessions. Although she is a bit younger than me, we clicked straightaway, and she is still my dear friend and confidante today, many years later. Unfortunately, it took me thirty minutes to drive to work, so when the offer of a job at Palm Beach came up, I couldn't say no. It was for a part-time marketing manager at the local RSL, and was located just five hundred metres from our home.

I loved advertising and marketing, loved a challenge, was passionate about the area and the role involved helping our local RSL improve its business. It was perfect for me! The essential element of the job was to 'put bums on seats' during the week.

It wasn't long before I had created 'A Day in Paradise'. I decided to target senior citizens and began marketing a day out for the residents of retirement villages and for senior citizens clubs throughout Sydney. A coach service would drop the visitors at the Church Point Wharf. I would then welcome them on board the ferry and we would set off on a morning-tea cruise on Pittwater. Back on land the coach would transport them to the RSL club for lunch. Afterwards I would take them on a guided tour of Palm Beach, including the filming location of *Home and Away*, the long-running national TV drama. I would give a running commentary, filling them in on the history of the area and local landmarks. It wasn't long before the club would have up to two or three coachloads of seniors in at any one time.

Putting together this commentary had been enlightening for me. I realised that I had a creativity in me that I hadn't been aware of. I created something from nothing and it was successful. I had sourced most of the information from old books I'd found at the club and some from books I had borrowed from locals. There didn't seem to be a comprehensive guide to the area. I was surprised. Palm Beach was a slice of paradise; surely the rest of the world should know about it? The seed of an idea began to form, which was to develop into the very first visitors' guide to the Northern Beaches of Sydney.

I started by taking notes every day. If I was to write a visitors' guide, what would it look like? I decided it needed to be small, so that it could fit in a handbag. It would have everything in it a visitor would need: editorials about all the best places to visit, accommodation, restaurants, tourist activities, shopping, transport and bus and ferry timetables. I began creating mock-ups on the computer. The more time I spent on it, the more real it became. *This is what the area needs, this could really take off,* I thought.

I started looking for ways to make the project happen. Paul and I certainly couldn't afford to produce the guide on our own. I found a little book called *The Marine Directory*, which was a similar concept marketed to the boating industry. I called the publisher, Bill, and met with him at his office. The meeting went well and Bill suggested we go into partnership. I hadn't thought of that, but it was a logical solution. I had no way of publishing the guide on my own, and he had the experience and gear that was needed. I left Bill's with a spring in my step. I couldn't believe it—here was little old me, someone who had never felt like I had achieved anything much in my life, and I was about to embark on a business venture that could change the shape of our future.

Bill and I spent a day discussing what the guide would look like, what the content would be and how many pages of advertising it would need to make a profit after costs. Bill would be responsible for putting the guide together, making all the ads and collating the first edition. I was to approach local businesses and sell the advertising, and Paul would do all of the photography. Bill's experience told him we only had six months to put the guide together to be ready for the tourist season at Christmas or we would lose money, so we had our work cut out for us.

Shortly after that meeting, I had something to show prospective advertisers. Paul had captured the perfect photo of a pelican on the water for the cover and I had sent Bill the ads I had designed on the computer. Bill had produced a small white book, the pelican on the front and a few pages of the mocked-up ads inside. It didn't look all that professional really, it was still an idea on paper, but I didn't mind. I was convinced this was going to work, and I guess I must have convinced businesses I approached too, as I began signing advertisers up at nearly every appointment I made. Before too long every advertising space was sold, designed and approved. We were ready to go to print!

The day the guide came back from the printer's was exciting but nerve-wracking—my first publication. It was something I had created from nothing and was very different from what I had achieved as a parent. I was almost trembling as I opened one of the boxes. I picked up the first book. There it was: *The Northern Beaches Visitors' Guide 2000*. The front cover looked amazing. Excitedly I opened the book to the first page. My excitement turned to dismay. It was upside down! Frantically we opened box after box, checking them all. Nearly every second book we came across had the same printer's error. My heart sank. How could this have happened? I was devastated. All we could do was salvage the ones that were intact, so we could at least get them out to the advertisers. We would have to sort through the entire 50,000 print run. Despite this setback, delivering the guide was so exciting and made me feel so proud. Everyone could see that it was going to benefit the businesses and the area. Bill got in touch with the printers, who agreed to reprint another 15,000 copies to make up for the error.

A few months later, after we had delivered the first edition, we wasted no time in preparing and selling the second edition. Bill had helped us learn what we needed to know and he didn't have the time to spend with us helping to put the new edition out, but now Paul and I were ready to go it alone. We decided to expand the guide to include colour maps and photographs. We also launched a website www.sydneynorthernbeaches.com.au as an online version of the guide. Over one hundred advertisers attended a function we had for the launch at Barrenjoey House in Palm Beach. This little white book with the pelican on the front cover was a hit. I was on cloud nine, confident the business could provide us with financial freedom.

•

Official photo with the *This is Your Life* book, August 1996. Teresa and her son Andrew, Patrick, Michael, Diana, Mum, Rebecca and me.

The afternoon after the filming of *This Is Your Life*. The family relaxing around the lounge at a rented apartment in Palm Beach. (Clockwise) Teresa and Andrew, Diana, Rebecca, Patrick, Michael and me.

Our first time together on Palm Beach headland where Corey played me 'The Last Post'. A most memorable day.

Corey and me. Our first photo together. What a joy!

The first time my three sons are together: Josh, Corey and Jem.

Rebecca, Diana and me sharing a laugh while preparing for my wedding to Paul at Palm Beach, Sydney, 24 January 1999.

Feeling like a princess, with my sister Diana, getting ready at Barrenjoey House, Palm Beach, Sydney, 24 January 1999.

Josh and me on my favourite 'fishing' rock on my wedding day at Palm Beach, 1999.

'The triangle is complete.' Meeting Corey's adoptive Mum, Carol, in New Zealand, 2000.

Trip to New Zealand to meet Corey's mum. What a special lady she is. Jem, me, Carol, Corey and Josh.

My three sons, New Zealand, 2000.

Teresa, me, Diana and Rebecca, Patrick's fiftieth birthday, Brisbane, 2007.

Patrick's fiftieth birthday, a great night. Gibney get-togethers are legendary.
Patrick, Diana, Michael, Rebecca, me, and Teresa.

My surprise fiftieth at Rebecca's in Clareville, Sydney, March 2010. The Gibneys doing what they do best: dancing, laughing and always having fun!

Family portrait taken at my surprise fiftieth, March 2010.

Rebecca and me before a charity ball in Melbourne, 2012. Special sister, special times.

Gift from Corey at our first family Christmas together, December 2013.

My gorgeous family, at the Newport Arms, December 2013. Josh, my soon-to-be-daughter-in-law, Claire, Jem, Corey, my daughter-in-law Sarah and me. Happy times!

I was in the kitchen preparing dinner one afternoon, when I heard Josh and Jem arrive home from school.

'Mum, you need to come and see Josh,' Jem called out with an urgency in his voice.

'What's wrong?' I called as I walked to the door to meet them.

Josh was standing there with his head bowed. 'I'm all right, Mum. I'm all right,' he said.

I bent down to look at him. I was horrified—he had a huge bruise on his upper cheek; his left eye was puffed up, and blood was dripping from his lips.

'What happened?' I said in fright, and quickly led him into the lounge room and sat him down on the couch.

'It was horrible, Mum,' Jem said. 'It was the boy who was expelled from our school, he punched Josh in the face when he got off the bus, I saw it all.' Jem was trying to hold back the tears.

I knew straightaway which boy Jem was talking about. The previous year, Josh had been bullied on several occasions. Discussing it with the school, we had decided to move Josh to another class. By the end of that year the boy had bullied several others and been expelled.

I needed to do something, this boy had to be stopped. When Paul got home, I asked him to take photos of Josh's injuries so I had evidence of the assault. I thought we should file charges, but that was Josh's decision to make, not mine. We spoke about it, and I told him that I felt if we did nothing this boy would keep intimidating and bashing people. I had that afternoon rung a number of parents at the school the boy now attended and been horrified to learn the behaviour was ongoing and many local kids were scared of him.

After lots of thought, Josh decided to file charges. He was only fifteen and this was a brave thing for him to do. We filled out a police report and were told we would be contacted by a social worker because the boys were under the age of sixteen. Jem also had to complete a report of the abuse, as he had been witness to it. A couple of weeks later, we received a letter stating we had to attend a mediation meeting. Apparently this was a new initiative to help children and young adults communicate with each other after a dispute. I felt sick to my stomach. I had encouraged Josh to file an assault charge, and now he had to face the boy who had assaulted him in a round-table discussion. I was angry, this felt wrong, but there was nothing I could do about it.

When we arrived at the meeting, which was held in a small room, the chairs were placed in a circle. We would all be facing each other. A policeman, a social worker, the boy who had assaulted Josh, his mother and his uncle were already seated. The remaining chairs were for Josh, Paul, myself and the principal of the school, who had come along as moral support for Josh.

We each had five minutes to share the impact the assault had had on our lives, and they had the opportunity to respond. I told of my devastation at seeing my son physically harmed. When it was Josh's turn, he looked directly at the boy. 'Why did you punch me?' he asked. 'I didn't do anything to deserve that.' I was proud of Josh, he was facing up to a boy he was scared of. The boy apologised. He seemed ashamed. Apparently he had been through a family tragedy and had resorted to taking his anguish out on others. It wasn't an excuse but it made the boy's behaviour more understandable. The whole incident hadn't been dealt with in the way I thought, but the outcome was good. Josh was free from fearing this boy and he had closure on the events of that day. I had talked to Josh about the importance of dealing with difficult events in life, of learning to forgive and move on with your life.

Chapter Twenty-four

By the time I started selling advertising for the third edition of the visitors' guide, our financial situation was becoming critical. Paul's photography work had really fallen away. The television network had continued to make cutbacks and he could no longer rely on a regular income. We had made enough on the second edition to cover costs, but there wasn't enough profit to live on. It was worrying and difficult for us both. Palm Beach was such an expensive place to live and we were now having to pay for Josh and Jem's private education. I had considered putting them in a public school but they had had so many changes in their lives and they had just started high school so I couldn't do it to them. We had to find a way.

Racking my brains for a solution, I remembered a conversation I had had with Michael and Moira when I had stayed with them in Melbourne. Even then I'd been full of dreams and ideas. Michael had encouraged me to follow my dreams and said if I ever needed the financial backing I should give them a call. At the time I had felt deeply encouraged by this—I had never had anyone believe in me like that. So I picked up the phone now and called. I filled Michael in about the guide, the website and my ideas for further expansion. He didn't hesitate. 'Of course I'll support you. It sounds like you're on a winner.' Michael became our lifeline and month after month he provided the funds we needed to keep going. He believed in me and I wasn't going to let him down. I plunged headlong into developing the business, often working twelve hours a day, seven days a week, out and about selling during the day. Nights and weekends I spent designing, collating, writing and doing the accounting. It was hard work, but we had a purpose and a vision.

It was around 5.30, one cold, wet winter's evening, and Paul and I were in the office working. The boys were upstairs playing a computer game, when suddenly I heard footsteps running down the wooden stairs leading to the office. 'Mum, Mum!' Jem called, running into the room in his pyjamas; he was breathless with excitement.

'What is it? What's so exciting?' I replied with a grin on my face, thinking he had just won a game against Josh.

'It's Dad, it's Dad. He's here, he's upstairs,' Jem said.

The smile slipped from my face. I couldn't believe what I was hearing. 'What do you mean, Dad is here?' I asked, hoping he was joking with me.

'He really is. Mum, you gotta come up and see,' Jem said, running back up the stairs.

I looked at Paul and felt the blood drain from my face. I thought I might faint. I had not seen Kieran since the day he came to collect the boys all those years ago in Brisbane.

'It's okay, I'm here,' Paul said reassuringly as we made our way up the stairs.

Kieran was waiting at the back door. He was shirtless, in black jeans and sandals, and was dripping wet. Oddly, he had a guitar slung over his back—as far as I knew, he didn't play the guitar. I greeted him nervously, managing to force a quiet 'Hello' out of my mouth. I was shaking, unsure why he was here. Was he angry? Was this payback time?

I introduced him to Paul while the boys ran around excitedly saying, 'Dad's here, Dad's here.'

'Come inside,' Paul said, and we made our way into the living room.

Jem was quick to jump up on his dad's lap, throwing his arms around him. 'It's so good to see you!'

It was nice to see Josh and Jem so excited, but I was still afraid. We asked him to stay for dinner, making small talk, all the while trying to determine his state of mind. Paul was great with him, asking questions and trying to make him feel comfortable. After dinner, Josh and Jem were showing Kieran around the house, when Jem came running back into the room. 'Mum, can Dad stay a few days? He has nowhere else to go, and it's cold and raining,' he pleaded.

What could I say? He looked so different from the man I had married. I looked at Paul: *What do we do?*

'Maybe just let him stay downstairs in the office for a night,' Paul replied.

We had a sofa bed downstairs, and a separate shower and toilet, so I thought it would be safe. Okay, I agreed, he could stay, but only overnight.

The next morning, the boys got up and ran down to see Kieran. It was a Saturday and so they didn't have school. After breakfast, Jem asked if he could go with his dad into the shops in Avalon.

'What for?' I asked.

'Dad just wants to go for a walk,' he replied.

I was nervous of letting him go and nervous of the possible consequences if I said no. Although Kieran seemed calm, I wasn't sure what was going on inside his head. I knew Jem wanted to go so I spoke with Paul and he said it would be fine.

'All right then, but only for a couple of hours,' I replied.

I didn't know what was right, but I let them go off together, praying Jem would be okay.

They did come back a few hours later and Jem seemed happy enough. 'Can Dad stay for a few more days?' he asked. I knew Kieran would have told Jem to ask on his behalf; he knew it would make it more difficult for me to say no if the boys asked. It was frightening to think of him staying on. Kieran seemed in control, but every so often I would catch him giving me such an angry look. I knew he was still furious with me, at how unfairly he felt he had been treated. I was worried the anger would erupt and he would take it out on me. I felt safe with Paul around, though, and for the boys' sake we agreed he could stay a couple more days.

The next day I was at the local shop picking up a few things and I overheard two women talking. 'Have you seen that guy who's hanging around Avalon?' one asked.

'No, which one?'

'There was a guy in Avalon yesterday, he didn't have a shirt on and he was playing a guitar and singing. He had a boy with him, about ten or eleven, and he was singing too. They had a hat in front of them on the pavement.'

I was stunned, they were talking about Kieran and Jem! Kieran had obviously taken Jem into Avalon to busk for money. The fact that he hadn't told me, and had obviously told Jem not to say anything either, meant he knew it wasn't right but he had done it anyway. I knew then that I couldn't trust him. The threatening looks he had been giving me had really started to rattle me, and they seemed to be occurring more often. I knew he had to leave but I didn't know what would happen if I asked him to go. At one point when Paul went to the kitchen Kieran glared at me, saying, 'You took my boys from me!'

I needed advice. I had been talking to Rebecca and had told her how worried I was that Kieran might explode. She had given me the number of a police officer, Mark, who had many years of experience dealing with people who suffered from mental illness. I had rung him straightaway, telling him of my experience with Kieran, and he had said to call him if Kieran's behaviour started to change. I got in the car and drove down the street to a phone box to call him. 'Hello Mark, it's Stella again, I'm so sorry to bother you but I need your advice.' My voice was shaking, I was scared now and Mark could tell. I filled him in on what had happened and how I was feeling about Kieran's behaviour towards me.

'I'm too scared to ask him to leave. What will he do? I –'

'Listen carefully,' Mark said, interrupting me. 'You need to take control of yourself. You cannot allow Kieran to see you scared. Get Paul to ask him to leave. If he doesn't, then my advice is to leave yourselves. It sounds as if he could be a time bomb waiting to explode. You don't want to be around if he does.' His voice was strong yet caring. 'And one last thing, you need to notify your local police station of what is going on and where you can be reached.'

I got off the phone and felt my body go weak. How could this be happening again? I had been told Kieran had been diagnosed with bipolar and prescribed medication however his behaviour would change dramatically when he wasn't taking it. I was sympathetic towards Kieran although I was concerned. The way he would look at me every now and then, with a look of anger in his eyes, I knew it wasn't right for him to stay any longer.

When I got home Paul went down to Kieran straightaway to tell him he needed to leave. When he came back upstairs he said Kieran had refused to go. I began to feel very afraid now and I knew we had to do what Mark had suggested and leave ourselves, but without Kieran realising what was going on. That night we packed a couple of bags and snuck them into the car in the dark before we went to bed.

Morning came. It was a school day, and Kieran came upstairs asking if he could have some food.

'No,' Paul said, trying to sound authoritative, 'we're going out for the day, and you need to leave before we get home this afternoon.'

Kieran glared at him. 'I'm not going anywhere.'

Paul didn't respond—we knew not to antagonise him—so we quietly finished tidying up, and after Kieran had gone back downstairs, we locked the front door and got in the car to leave. Josh and Jem both ran over to hug their dad goodbye. It must have been so hard for Josh and Jem to say goodbye to their dad but they knew he wasn't well and was acting strangely.

'Come on, boys, you'll be late for school,' Paul called.

On the way to school I tried to explain that we wouldn't be going home tonight and that we needed to stay somewhere else until Dad had gone. It was hard. The boys always struggled between loving their dad but also knowing something wasn't right with his behaviour.

We booked into accommodation close to the school and far enough away from Palm Beach and Kieran. We ended up having to stay for four nights before we knew Kieran had finally left our home and the area. I was lucky that I had been able to reach Steve, Kieran's friend from the Gold Coast. He had told us Kieran was angry but was hitchhiking back to Queensland.

It was safe to go home now, but what if Kieran changed his mind and came back to Sydney again? I was still nervous.

The next day, the phone rang and Jem ran to answer it. 'Hi Dad,' he said with surprise. My stomach started doing flips. Jem didn't say much, except, 'I love you too,' before calling out 'Hey Josh, Dad wants to speak to you.' Josh took the phone and, like Jem, didn't say much, just appeared to be listening. At one point he dropped his head and looked really upset. 'I'm sorry, Dad, I'm sorry,' he said and he began to cry.

After he'd hung up, he ran to his room. I followed him. 'What did your dad say, Josh? What did he say to make you so sad?' I asked, trying to hold back my own tears.

Josh was distraught. I put my arms around him and held him tight. 'It's okay, Josh, I'm here. You don't have to tell me, but I'm here if you want me,' I said, trying to reassure him.

I sat there holding him until the crying eased.

'Dad blames me,' he said. All I could do that day was reassure Josh how special he was and how much we all loved him. I wasn't going to make any excuses for Kieran—I had done that for too many years—this time he had really gone too far. I couldn't fix this. Kieran would have to deal with the consequences and fix the damage himself.

As hard as it was to listen to Josh's pain, I was thankful that he felt he could share it with me. He was a teenager now, an age when children notoriously shut out their parents. For a while now I had been talking to the boys about my journalling and how it helped me. I had begun teaching them the importance of sharing their feelings, by talking, or drawing, or writing.

After Kieran's unexpected visit to Sydney, I noticed a change in the boys' behaviour. They would often fight with each other; sometimes it was playful, and sometimes, when one had upset the other, it would be a bit more aggressive. I tended to let them sort it out by themselves; however, after Kieran's visit the fighting became more serious. Josh's anger seemed out of control. It worried me. I sat him down and said, 'I'm concerned about how angry you seem when you fight with Jem. I have a hunch that it's not really him you're angry with. Am I right?' Josh was silent, his head down. 'Has this got anything to do with your dad?'

'I'm not sure,' he said.

I suggested he spend a bit of time thinking about things in his room. I suggested that if it was about his dad, he try writing him a letter. He could put down everything he had ever wanted to say to him. Especially the bits he would be afraid to say. We could post it or not, it would be his call. I left him to think things over.

A little later I popped my head around the door. He was writing furiously, and crying. I held back my own tears as I went over and hugged him. 'It'll be okay, Josh, keep going.' I kept checking on him, hugging and encouraging him each time until he had finished. He looked shattered. He gave me the letter to read. It was six pages long. I started to cry as I read it, my poor son's pain was evident. He had written so well. I was relieved for him that he had been able to express himself but distraught that he was so sad. We cried together. Afterwards Josh said he wasn't angry any more and he actually felt a bit better. How proud I was of him, facing the pain and starting to let it go.

Jem expressed his emotions differently. He didn't seem angry, in fact he had been quieter than normal, withdrawing into himself. This was Jem's way of dealing with conflict and pain. A week or so after my chat with Josh, I spoke with Jem. I explained how much better Josh had felt after writing the letter. I suggested it might be a good idea for him as well. I left him with a notepad and pen. I checked on him and saw that he had started to write. Even though I could see he had been crying, he said, 'I'm okay, Mum.' He wanted to be left alone. When he had finished, I sat with him, and although he had been crying, he seemed relieved.

His letter was long, and as painful as Josh's to read. Both boys turned a corner after their letters to their dad. Neither wanted them to be sent to him. They had expressed their feelings, that was enough.

To this day I still feel terribly sad about my relationship with Kieran and how it unfolded. There are always two sides to every story and I know I played my part in the breakdown of our marriage. There were many issues we had to deal with and we married so very young. I can only hope that he is happy in his life now.

Chapter Twenty-five

After two and a half years of supporting the visitors' guide, Michael called to say that he couldn't back the business any longer, that I needed to make it work on my own now.

When he explained the figures to me, I was shocked. I knew the costs of producing the guide were high, but I had assumed we were keeping ahead of things. Michael wasn't blaming me or wanting to make me feel bad, he was just giving me the facts.

'I had no idea it had been that much. I am so sorry, Michael. I will do everything I can to pay you back,' I replied, trying to sound in control even though I was shaking inside.

After I got off the phone I felt sick, I wanted to cry, I wanted to run away from it all. I pulled myself together.

I have to make this work, I told myself. *I will sell as much advertising as I can, and make a bigger profit than last year, so we can start repaying Michael.* I was convincing myself it would be okay.

We were now under real financial stress. Paul's photography work wasn't earning anywhere near a real income. He had been helping me with the business but was at a loss as to how to generate any other funds. The strain was beginning to tell on our relationship. We had been through so much, but the money worries caused all sorts of silly arguments and these escalated with time. I was worried about what effect this was having on my boys. Arguments again!

There was a distance between us now that was not there before. There was no closeness, no intimacy; the stress and strain of the financial pressure seemed to be affecting every area of our relationship and we were almost strangers living in the same house. A few months later Paul and I separated. It was hard being alone again, but I had to look after my boys. I didn't want them to go through the same anguish they had years earlier of listening to all the arguments. They had been through so much and I was determined to protect them. I had to provide for them. I was going to do my best to make the business work. Firstly, I knew I had to reduce my outgoings, starting with the rent. I couldn't leave the area—my advertisers were there, along with the boys' friends and school. But I couldn't afford to stay in Palm Beach. Mona Vale was only a short distance away and I managed to find a great unit there. We were on the move, again! The boys loved the new location even more. It was still close to the beach, but as they were older now, they loved being in a busier environment.

The next few months I spent selling advertising on the next edition, while furiously trying to chase unpaid invoices from the year before. I was able to keep our heads above water financially, but only just. I was beginning to realise the guide could not support itself. Costs were rising, but the advertisers were struggling with the global financial crisis, and I had to keep the advertising price attractive. I needed to diversify. I had to find alternative ways to bring more revenue into the business. I put on my thinking cap.

First off was rebranding, extending across Australia and New Zealand. The website for the guide had been online since 2001. Page views had increased each year, both locally and overseas. Visitors to the site were often downloading the bus and ferry timetables we had made available. My vision was to expand the existing website to a community portal, one that had every business on the Northern Beaches listed on it. Businesses could buy space on the website for a set-up and then annual fee. Restaurant owners could have menus on the site; tradies could have an affordable website with before and after shots of their work; locals could order takeaways and make bookings online. My mind was buzzing with all the possibilities. This website would be a one-stop shop for locals and tourists. Everything you needed to know, all in the one place. I knew I would have to come up with a name to encompass all the website had to offer.

I enlisted Jem's help. He has a creative mind, and I knew he could help me come up with the right domain name for the business. We spent the night brainstorming, until suddenly he thought of it. 'What about "Where I live"?' It sounded perfect, and it was simple. We went online to check the availability; the domain name had already been taken but wasn't online. Maybe we could try 'Where we live?' There it was, available, and I registered it straightaway. Right, what next?

I had established a need for trades and services and restaurant guides separate to the visitors' guide. The trades and services guide would be black and white to keep costs down for the advertisers. We could also sell the web space at the same time. If they bought a display ad in the guide we would reduce the web page fee. The restaurant guide was to be in full colour and divided into locations. Both the guides would be distributed free throughout the Northern Beaches. I worked out the advertising rates, together with costing, and the revenue from both guides would make us a good profit! I was buzzing.

A short time later I met Helen, a bookkeeper. I had struggled with the administrative side of the business from the beginning. I was the ideas person, but I needed a business brain. Helen fitted the bill. I knew I wasn't in a position to pay her, but we agreed to work something out over time.

Helen could see the potential of my ideas and was keen to be involved. We put our heads together and came up with a plan. Helen had some money put aside and wanted to help get things going, so we had the resources to produce mock guides for selling and a new logo for the rebrand. I didn't have to resume selling on the visitors' guide until September. It was now May. I had four months to sell. I was used to the pressure, I was going to do this!

Helen reined me in. We could both see that it would be too much for one person. We decided we needed to recruit sales staff, operating on retainer plus commission. We would also need premises to work from as my unit wasn't big enough. Within three weeks we had an office in Warriewood and three sales people. It was my role to train and equip them with everything they needed to make the sale. We employed them on a three-month trial basis. Two were experienced; the third had a winning personality. We had three months, it was going to be hard. I wasn't prepared for their performance, however. All I heard at the end of the working week was, 'It's a slow market,' and, 'Businesses don't want to risk advertising in something they can't see.' They just didn't have the passion I had. How could they? They didn't have the vision. Helen was less than impressed—her investment was being swallowed up by their retainers. One by one, we had to let them go. We had no advertising revenue and the guides would not be going to print. Helen stopped coming into the office. Her emails were understandably becoming more and more irate. She had invested so much money and wanted to be paid.

One day Helen stormed into the office and dumped her account books onto the desk. She wanted nothing more to do with the business. I understood her anger. She had invested in me and the vision I had. I had let another person down.

I was devastated. Every person who had believed in me, I had let down. I had failed in two marriages. My business was failing. I had failed. I was a failure.

I drove home in tears. I knew what I needed to do, before anything else, and that was to write in my journal. I hadn't written for a while, as I had been frantically busy trying to keep the business afloat. *I am a failure*, I wrote over and over again. All my life I had tried to do the right thing and it always ended up wrong, wrong, wrong! Why did God let this happen to me? I thought he loved me.

I was crying and writing furiously. Eventually I started to understand that God still loved me. And then I saw the picture in my head. The heart and the arrows. There was the fourth arrow with God's name on the fletching. It had dropped to the ground. I had cried and written my way through to realising it wasn't God's fault. It was just what happened. Seasons come and then they go. I was still here and I was still loved. It was an incredible moment. I was set free from blame. I shut my journal and felt peace.

•

The next day I knew I had choices. I could feel sorry for myself or I could do something about it. I decided to do what I could to salvage the business. I had two boys to provide for and Michael and now Helen who I wanted to pay back. I was not going to give up.

I knew I had to get back into selling the visitors' guide and generate an income. I realised I needed help to get the revenue coming in faster. I would employ a commission-only sales person. That way I wouldn't have to pay a salary, only a percentage of what was sold. I still needed a space to work from, so I moved out of the bigger office into a tiny office in the same building. It was really only a cupboard, with room for one desk and a chair, but it would do. On my first day in the cupboard, Josh called in after school. He had written me a note to stick on my computer: *It's not who you are, it's just what you do. It's only work.* How precious that was and how much it meant to me. My own dear son was reminding me what was important in life.

I contacted an employment agency to assist me in recruiting a sales rep. Alice, the owner of the agency, came to my office herself to discuss my requirements. It wasn't long before I was sharing with Alice my vision for the business—I couldn't help myself, the passion was still there! Alice was enthusiastic. She said she had money to invest and we could form a company. This could be the answer I was looking for. I was determined to make it work. I liked Alice; she seemed honest and we got on well together, so what could go wrong?

Over the next few weeks we formed a company. It seemed fitting to call it Where Publishing. Alice bought a 35-per-cent share in the business and her brother, who was a silent partner, bought 10 per cent. The remaining 55 per cent belonged to me. From the sale of those shares we had enough to keep the business operational for the next six months, plus I could pay some outstanding debts from my previous sole trader business. It kept the wolf from the door, but I still owed the printers, graphic designers and the tax department, not to mention Michael, Helen and a couple of other friends. I tried not to think about it. I just needed to keep positive and work hard to pay it all back.

Chapter Twenty-six

Josh had left school and was doing a mechanic's apprenticeship. He decided to buy himself a decent car and he managed to secure a loan from the bank to buy a sports car. I tried to talk him out of it, I really didn't want him to have a car too powerful. I had taught both boys to drive and, although he wasn't a reckless driver, Josh had a love for speed that worried me.

Very early one morning, around 1 am, my phone rang and disturbed me from a deep sleep. Both boys were out for the night, Jem was staying at a friend's and Josh was meeting his friend Kelsey to show him his new car. I woke with a start, immediately alarmed. 'Hello,' I answered in a croaky voice.

'Mrs Page! Mrs Page!' screamed a voice down the phone. Page was the boys' last name; I had reverted to my maiden name, but their friends always called me Mrs Page and I never corrected them. 'It's Josh! He's been in an accident!'

My heart began to pound. 'Is that you, Kelsey?'

'Yes,' he said, his voice still frantic.

I tried to stay calm but my body had started to shake with fear. 'Kelsey, please, you have to calm down and tell me what has happened.'

'Josh was in an accident. He spun out of control on a bend, hit a fence and he has blood coming from the back of his head.'

I was trembling violently now. 'Where are you? Have you called the ambulance? Or the police?' He said he hadn't. I asked whether Josh was conscious; he was. 'That's good, Kelsey. Now, is Josh there? Can I speak to him?' The phone went quiet for a second.

'Mum, Mum, I crashed the car! I crashed the car!' he repeated.

'It's okay, Josh, I'm on my way.' I asked Josh to put Kelsey back on the phone. I could tell my son was in shock.

'Kelsey, I will call the ambulance and the police, but I am on my way, he will be okay.' I was trying to reassure Kelsey without knowing myself whether my son was going to survive this.

I immediately phoned the police. 'Please, can you send a police car to the Pacific Highway near the Seventh Day

Adventist Hospital.' Kelsey had described the location of the crash to me. 'My son has just been in an accident and there is no one on the scene. Can you arrange an ambulance? I'm not sure what state Josh is in, please hurry, please hurry.' I didn't stop for a breath, I was panicking now.

'Please try and calm down. We will send a car immediately,' was the reply.

I hung up the phone and frantically dressed in trackpants and a sweater. I was shaking as I started the car. I began to pray, and I kept praying for the entire long drive to the Pacific Highway. I knew roughly where on the highway they would be. As I came around a bend, I could see flashing red lights. My heart was racing. There was a tow truck in the middle of the road and the wreckage of the car, but no sign of Josh or Kelsey.

Frantically I parked the car and ran across the road to the tow truck driver. 'Where is he? Where is he?' I was screaming. I looked over the tow truck driver's shoulder and saw the car properly. It was a crumpled mess. The entire back of the vehicle had concertinaed almost up to the front seats; the doors were buckled and there was glass everywhere. I felt sick inside.

'He's okay,' the driver reassured me. 'The ambulance came and they've taken him to Hornsby hospital. You gotta know, your son was very lucky tonight. Someone was watching over him, because you would be burying him if he'd been any closer to that pole.' He pointing to black tyre marks on the road. They stopped centimetres short of a power pole.

'Thank you, God,' I whispered.

I arrived at Hornsby hospital to find Josh in the emergency ward. He was sitting on a bed with his head in his hands. All he could say was, 'I'm sorry, I'm sorry.'

I put my arms around him. He was in shock still, but he was alive and I was so grateful. All he had suffered were minor cuts and concussion. It was a miracle.

Afterwards, there was a lot for Josh to deal with. He wasn't insured. The loan he had taken out on the car still needed to be repaid. He had a vehicle he could no longer drive, and he couldn't afford a replacement. He even found he couldn't get behind the wheel of any vehicle. It was some time before the trauma subsided. He needed time to get over the accident.

•

The business seemed to be going well at last. We had published the latest visitors' guide and it continued to be well received. Alice and I decided to implement our next idea, the voucher book. Each year the visitors' guide had a section in which local businesses could offer their customers a discount voucher. We decided to put these vouchers together into a separate book so it would be another form of advertising. I had already built up a good rapport with local businesses and knew it would be easy to sell. It only took a few months before we had enough subscribers to go to print. We were impressed when the book came back from the printers, full colour, with all the vouchers individually perforated. The user could take out a single voucher without ruining the page. There were vouchers for everything—restaurants, shopping discounts, and discounts on activities, transport and more. We were sure this book would do well. Unfortunately, we were relying on the schools to assist us in distribution, but discovered too late that they were already committed to an entertainment book, which was the same concept as ours but not local. Had they been approached earlier they would have preferred ours. Lesson learned. We did manage to sell enough books to cover costs, but it made a serious dent in the budget.

We needed to cut expenses, so we stopped paying ourselves a wage. It was then that I made a terrible mistake. Without any other source of income, I had to keep paying rent and we had to eat. I was desperate. I decided to sell some of my shares to Alice. It would buy me a few weeks to figure something out. Those few weeks went by and of course the bank account dwindled. I knew I couldn't sell any more shares, I was already realising the stupidity of giving up control of the company. I decided my only option was to find part-time work, to earn enough to live on.

Luckily, my previous employer at the Palm Beach RSL was happy to take me back. I would work four days a week selling advertising on the visitors' guide and a new publication we were trialling, the *Coastal Bride*, then head to the RSL for one day in marketing, then reception work Friday and Saturday nights, and all day Sunday. It sounds busy and it was, but I loved the RSL team, they were almost like family to me. I was also grateful to be earning an income that allowed me to at least pay rent every week.

Over time, though, I struggled to make my part-time income cover all the bills. I was slipping behind in my rent and I still had outstanding debts, one of which had recently resulted in a summons to court. I was overwhelmed. I didn't know what to do. I made an appointment to see the crisis centre at St Vincent de Paul. I had heard they would provide free financial advice for people in hardship. I went in to see them and laid it all on the table, taking all of my bills from my sole trader business with me. Their advice was blunt: file for bankruptcy. Bankruptcy! Me! I couldn't believe it. I had been convinced that I could turn it all around and start to pay everybody back. It was obvious now that this wasn't going to happen and in the meantime the debt would only increase to insurmountable proportions. It was one of the hardest things I have ever had to do, but I took their advice. I filed. My journals at that time reflect my feelings of utter helplessness, shame and guilt. I thought it was the worst moment of my life but there were more to come.

•

It was a Friday morning and I was tired but on a high. The previous night we had staged the Miss Palm Beach final. The competition had been my initiative and it was a huge success in terms of patronage and status for the RSL club. It was a rewarding feeling having come up with the idea and making it happen. At a time when I was feeling I wasn't much of a success in life, it reminded me that some of my ideas were good ones.

When I arrived at the office Alice was at her desk. 'We need to talk,' she said straightaway, as if she was in a hurry to get the words out.

'Sure, what do we need to talk about?' I asked, thinking she had an idea for the business.

'It's not working,' she said.

'What do you mean? What's not working?' I was wondering what on earth she was referring to.

'I have to let you go.'

'What do you mean, let me go?' I asked blankly. Then the penny dropped. 'Are you firing me from my own business?' I could only hope she was playing some sick joke on me.

I was stunned. Immediately I thought of the shares I had sold her. I had handed over the power to Alice. 'You can't fire me, I'm the business. This is my baby, I started it from nothing. Everything I have done in the last twelve years has been to make this business successful, and now you want to take it from me. Why? What have I done to deserve this?'

'I think you need to go and work somewhere else for a while.'

How dare she! I was working as hard as was humanly possible to keep the business going. Alice was trying to protect what we had both put into the business. It was a complicated business situation, whereby we were both owed money by the business.

'I need you to hand over your keys to the office and your laptop,' she said.

I was so shocked and upset, I began to cry.

Alice came over and tried to hug me, but I lost it. Usually I would back down in any conflict. I hated confrontation. I had been through enough in my life and I avoided it at all costs. Alice knew this and was as surprised as I was at my reaction.

'Don't touch me! Don't you dare try and patronise me!' I grabbed my bag and fled. At that moment I felt as though my whole world had fallen apart. Driving home I couldn't stop crying. Every so often I had to pull over to the side of the road to wipe my eyes. I felt like someone had ripped open my heart and stolen the very inside of me.

I finally made it home and went to my room. 'God, why? Why have you allowed this to happen? I felt sure you had given me the dream. I felt sure you had told me to hold on to it when times got tough. Why are you doing this to me?'

I couldn't stop crying and spent the rest of the day in tears. Whenever I tried to calm myself, it would strike me again that I had lost everything. The business had been my life and my dream. Its success would mean I could pay back the people who had invested in me, and I would have something to pass on to my boys. It had all been taken away from me that day. In the midst of all this, the real estate agent rang to tell me I had fallen two weeks behind in my rent. 'Oh God, what am I going to do?'

The next morning I knew I needed to write in my journal. I had no more tears left to cry. I felt numb.

God, I know the Bible says you work all things together for good but right now I can't see where you are leading me. I am desperate to hear what you are saying to me. I held on to a dream for so long and now it has been taken away from me. It is totally out of my hands and I don't know what to do . . . All I know is I need to keep my heart from resenting Alice, to forgive her for hurting me and taking everything away from me. I just read a Bible verse, looking for something to encourage me and I opened it to Psalm 30: 'You turned my wailing into dancing.'

Of course, the journalling calmed me again, although it was going to take me a long time to forgive Alice. The next day I found a letter she had dropped off. She wrote that she was sorry for hurting me but it had been a necessary step. I think she believed she was doing the right thing. Maybe it was because I had filed for bankruptcy as a sole trader, and they may have come after the publishers to get the money they owed me in wages to pay my debtors. I wasn't sure, but the thought crossed my mind. I wasn't ready to read the letter right then, I was still angry. Then I was sad, then I was angry again. This went on for weeks. Eventually I realised I had to forgive her and let it go. I have learned in my life not to allow what someone does to me to affect the way I am as a person. I don't want to become bitter. 'Let it go,' I said to myself. 'Move on.'

I knew that I had successfully done that when Alice approached me about eighteen months later, asking if I would return on a commission-only basis. I arranged to meet with her, wondering how it would go. Would there be any bad feeling? After a few moments of awkwardness, the meeting went really well. I was still passionate about all my ideas, but I decided I couldn't go back. Still, it was good to know I had forgiven Alice, I was free. It is sad to see the guide is no longer being published. When I look back, I see that my drive and passion was what kept it going. That couldn't be replicated by anyone, I guess.

I was still coming to terms with everything, putting a smile on my dial, head down, keeping going, when a letter arrived in the post. It was from the real estate agent saying the house we lived in was going on the market. We needed to find somewhere else to live—again! When the boys came home that night I sat them down and explained. They looked at one another, then at me. 'Actually, Mum,' Josh said quietly,

'Jem and I have talked about finding a place of our own sometime. If it's okay with you, we could do it now.'

I could see Josh was finding it hard to say this; he was watching me, waiting for my reaction. I tried to keep my expression calm, but inside I was thinking, *Not now! I need you both. Don't go, you can't leave me!* Of course I didn't say that. 'What a wonderful idea,' I said. 'That's so great.' I meant it too. They were twenty-one and twenty-three, it was time for them to do their own thing. I was lucky to have had them around for this long. I put my arms around them, reassuring them, 'I'll be fine.'

They moved into a great two-bedroom flat in Newport. I was able to give them quite a bit of furniture—I didn't need it all as I had managed to find a granny flat in Mona Vale, not far away. They settled in quickly and loved their independence. I certainly hadn't curbed their activities at home, but it was a whole new experience for them looking after themselves. They thrived, and we saw each other often.

Meanwhile I had the old empty nest syndrome to cope with. I missed the constant activity, the boys and their friends.

So, what to do? I had lost my business, and I had to find a new home for my companion of five years, Jada, a staffy we had had since a puppy. Keep going, it's just another season. I could always journal.

Chapter Twenty-seven

It seems fitting that I write the final chapter while sitting overlooking the ocean on a cloudless summer's day on Mona Vale beach. Just a short stroll from here is my new flat. It was advertised as a beach shack, which describes it perfectly. It's one bedroom, with wooden floorboards and white shutters. It's equipped with all the mod cons and a frangipani tree overhangs the entrance—it's simply perfect.

After leaving the business I started looking for full-time employment and was offered a job in retail by a man I met through working at the club in Palm Beach. He owns several retail outlets. It was a good job and was just a short two-minute drive from home. The best part was having a regular income. For the first time in years I didn't have to worry about whether I could pay the rent.

After three years I began to feel a little restless, and although I enjoyed meeting people every day, I wanted to do something more challenging, a job where I could use some of the skills I had learned over the years. One of the roles I enjoyed in the business was organising the annual cocktail function for advertisers.

I am grateful to have had that experience and the opportunity it gave me to build good relationships with my clients, which is one of the reasons I now have a great job in event management. It is a varied role but my main responsibility is to organise functions and events. The most rewarding part of the job is to see a happy couple enjoying their wedding reception after spending months helping them plan the perfect day. The location is the icing on the cake, overlooking the ocean with views from every angle. It's simply magic.

These last three to four years have been some of the best of my life, with several memorable experiences that have made my heart sing.

One of these occasions was a surprise trip to China. One day I received an unexpected phone call from my friend Shelley's husband Mark. Shelley and Mark had moved to China for business seven years earlier and although we don't get to see each other often, we have a strong friendship that has lasted the distance. Mark had rung to tell me they were going to pay for a return air ticket to China for fourteen days for me to spend some time with Shelley. I could not believe it. I had never been anywhere other than New Zealand and was totally taken aback by their generosity. Needless to say I had a wonderful time catching up with them.

But it didn't stop at one trip. Last January I received a call from Shelley this time. 'Guess what?' she said excitedly. 'We want to pay for you to come and visit us here in Macau for your birthday.' I was beside myself, and to this day feel so totally blessed to have such an amazing friend in Shelley. I only hope one day I can bless her and the many others that have blessed me throughout the years in the same way.

The birthday surprises didn't stop there. I had another surprise coming my way. It was a birthday I will never forget, my surprise fiftieth, which my gorgeous sister Rebecca organised for me. We were supposed to be going out for a special lunch. I had been given a hint that it was on the water. Rebecca knows I love the ocean so I was sure she had organised a boat to take us to a waterside restaurant like Cottage Point Inn or somewhere similar. I was convinced I had figured it out when I asked her how I should dress. 'Dress lightly because it's warm, but bring a jacket,' were her instructions. I was convinced that that was it—I needed a jacket for the salt spray off the ocean on our trip over.

Rebecca picked me up around 11.30, telling me we just needed to call in to her place to pick up Richard and see Zac because he wanted to give me a gift, all of which sounded plausible. That was, until I started to make my way down the stairs into their living room. At the bottom of the stairs Richard was looking up at me. 'Happy birthday,' he said smiling. Why did he have a video camera in his hand? I didn't think much of it, that was just Richard wanting to capture the moment of Zac presenting me with a gift to remember the day by. But then as I stepped onto the third-last step I noticed balloons with brightly coloured ribbons hanging from the ceiling. One last step, and I was excited to see my sons standing there to greet me. Then as I turned to the left, I saw a sea of faces—my entire family all lined up in a circle. They begain singing 'Happy birthday to you, happy birthday, dear Stella, happy birthday to you.' I couldn't hold back the tears as I walked around the room embracing each of my siblings and my mum. I could not believe it. I was overwhelmed.

We spent the afternoon laughing and reminiscing while drinking champagne and eating gourmet food on the deck. By nightfall we were doing what us Gibneys always love to do and that is dance! It was the best way to end the most memorable birthday I have ever had. And I will be forever grateful to my wonderful sister Rebecca and my awesome sister-in-law Annie for organising it for me.

I have always loved Christmas, but Christmas Day 2013 was one I will hold very dear memories of. For this was the very first Christmas I was able to share with all three of my sons. Corey and his wife Sarah arrived on 20 December and stayed with me for the week, and although I had to work most days, we were able to hang out together in the evenings. Christmas Day was the most memorable for me as we gathered beside the Christmas tree, passing gifts to each other. Corey wanted to go first. 'This is something I would have given you for Christmas when I was about five years old,' he said, passing me a small gift wrapped in white tissue paper. Tears filled my eyes when I unravelled the paper to reveal the most beautiful small heart-shaped stone, painted bright red and shiny with the words 'Mum' inscribed on the front. It's hard to describe how special I felt at that moment, and what this Christmas meant to me to have my sons all together. It was magic. Today that rock takes pride of place on my bookshelf next to the photos of my three sons.

That was not the only special moment Corey and I have shared this last year. I started writing this manuscript in February 2013 and although I worked on it every weekend, it was hard finding time to dedicate to it while working full time. I needed time off to write, so that's what I did. I took ten days off and headed to New Zealand and stayed with my sister Diana. We had a special time together. I would sit at one end of the table writing furiously while dear Diana would be busy editing at the other end of the table in between making meals and pouring me coffee to keep me awake. I don't know how I did it but I managed to write 35,000 words in just nine days. I am so very grateful to my dear sis for that, and I am sure I would not have been able to finish this book if it wasn't for that time with her.

My stay in New Zealand was also special for another reason. It was Corey's birthday while I was there and my sister invited them down to share lunch with us. I wanted to do something special for him as it was the first birthday we had spent together. I couldn't afford an extravagant gift and knew that wasn't what would be important to him so I baked him the first birthday cake I had ever made for him. It wasn't the best looking cake and definitely not something to write home about, but it was made with love and that was special to Corey. Diana also suggested we spend some time together so Corey could read a little of my manuscript. So we sat next to each other as Corey read the first pages about his birth and the pain I felt giving him up to the joys of being reunited for the very first time at Sydney airport over sixteen years ago. These are memories I will hold close to my heart forever.

In summary, my life has been somewhat like an unfinished jigsaw puzzle with pieces scattered all over the place just waiting for the right moment to be put in place. Today I can say I am grateful to everyone in my life who played a part in helping me to put that puzzle together. At times it has been extremely painful and other times overwhelmingly joyous. But today all of the pieces of my life are back together and it feels good.

Some might say I have lived an extraordinary life. Some of you may think I have made some of this up. I didn't. I have five brothers and sisters who can verify it all. There have even been episodes I have left out! Writing all this has been an incredible journey for me. I have, for the first time, seen end to end the story of my life.

Throughout it all I have had my two beautiful boys, the lights of my life, my reason for carrying on each and every day. I currently have no man in my life. For a long time, I have had no need of one. Who knows, one day that might change. For now, I have a quiet life. I am still on the Northern Beaches. Not waterfront, but I can go there when I need to. The water still feeds my soul. I have a great job where I get to meet people every day and although I don't earn a lot it's enough to pay my now manageable bills. I see my boys for what we call 'family night' once a week, and they are both doing well. Josh recently proposed to his beautiful girlfriend of four years, Claire, and I am looking forward to a wedding next year. Jem is also in a loving relationship. The close bond with my mum, brothers and sisters still remains and when we all get together it's a riot. I have good friends that have stood by me through all the challenges I have faced along the way and I have another cute canine companion, Lucy, an eleven-year-old Shitzu.

From season to season, journalling and my faith have seen me through. Thanks for coming along for the ride.

Two years ago my gorgeous son Jem wrote and recorded this incredibly moving song for me. I hope you enjoy it as much as I do.

Jem's song: 'In Case It's Been a While'

I just wanna take time out this morning,
To express something that I don't express too often
My appreciation
For the only woman that's been there through every tribulation
And trial, she did it all with a smile
And I know things got a little shit for a while
But you pulled us out
Even managed to hold it all together when Dad walked out
And I don't know how you did it
But I know I probably would have turned out shittier if you didn't
And that goes for Josh too
We'd have given up anything in the world before we lost you
You're the only thing that's always been there
With a smile and a hug and an open ear
So I just wrote you a letter to say
You've got my love and respect and gratitude forever.

This ain't just coz you're my own mother
I've met a lot of mums, and no other

Has come from a broken home
And managed to raise two mature grown men on her own
That's a hell of a feat
Especially when you went through shit
That I'm not gonna repeat on beat,
But suffice to say,
You had a tougher childhood than we did,
I maintain that the main reason that I'm here today
Is that you taught me, what did you say?
'It's just a season . . .'.
Your refusal to fail is the main reason
That when things got really dark
And it felt like my whole world was falling apart
I pressed on to look for better days
So I wrote you this letter just to say
Thank you.

S is for the strength you possess;
to have a mother like you, we were blessed.
T is for the time that you spent doing your best
trying to build a stable home out of a mess.
E is for every time that you made us laugh
(even when you didn't mean to).
L is for the loads of shit that we've been through
L is also for the love that we mean to
Always show you—the rest the A.
Stella, Mum, at the end of the day

it doesn't matter what we call you, or where we live,
you've got two grown kids
who could never have turned out better
if it weren't for you. So I wrote you this letter
just in case it's been a while since I said it,
I love and appreciate you, and don't ever forget it.
Love Jem

<https://soundcloud.com/jem-page/
jem-in-case-its-been-a-while>

Acknowledgements

Thank you to the team at Allen & Unwin for making this experience possible, with special mention to Claire Kingston. Without her belief in me and my story this book would not have been possible.

Thank you also to Siobhán Cantrill for all of your hard work in helping to guide the book through production. And thanks to the rest of the team who have been hard at work behind the scenes putting this book together; for your efforts I will be forever grateful.

A special thanks to Michael and Moira for welcoming us into your home in Melbourne many years ago and for the financial support you so freely gave. I have been truly humbled by your generosity and hope one day I can repay you for your kindness.

To my dearest friend Shelley, who has been like another sister to me, I am so grateful to have you in my life and I look forward to sharing old age together.

To Raelene, who I have known for over 25 years, thank you for always encouraging me to have faith and believe in my dreams.

There are many other friends I have made over the years whom I have not mentioned but I am thankful to each and every one of you for sharing your lives with me.

Thank you also to my fabulous siblings, for always being there and for loving me. To my beautiful sister Rebecca, thank you for your constant love and friendship throughout the years. If it wasn't for you this book would never have been possible. To my gorgeous sister Diana, partner in crime. Thank you so much for all your help with the editing; I couldn't have done it without you. I am truly grateful to have such a wonderful family. We have an incredible bond, and I love you all to bits.

Thanks to my amazing mum. Words cannot express how much I love you and how thankful I am for the constant love and support you have shown me throughout my life. No matter what you have always been there for me. I will be forever grateful. You taught me one of the most powerful principles in life and that is to forgive, which has helped set me free to be myself.

Finally, I want to thank my beautiful sons, Corey, Josh and Jem, and their gorgeous partners, Sarah and Claire. To

Corey, thank you so much for freely forgiving me for giving you up as a baby and taking the courageous steps to come to Australia to meet me and your brothers sixteen years ago. I am so glad we now have you in our family.

To Josh and Jem, who gave me the strength to get up every day and inspired me to keep going. You have been through so much over the years and yet you both remain true to yourselves, being the most kind and gentle human beings on the planet. Josh, you have been a rock, to not only me, but to everyone who knows you. You are a giver and carer. Everyone who knows you is touched by your kindness. Jem, your kind and gentle spirit warms the hearts of people you come into contact with. Your generous nature is a rare and beautiful quality. Words cannot adequately express how truly blessed I feel to have the privilege to have raised you as my sons and how very proud I am of the men you have become. I will love you with all my heart forever.